THE
LITTLE BOOK OF

ANCIENT ROME

TOM
SYKES

summersdale

THE LITTLE BOOK OF ANCIENT ROME

An Hachette UK Company
www.hachette.co.uk

Summersdale Publishers
Part of Octopus Publishing Group Limited
Carmelite House
50 Victoria Embankment
LONDON
EC4Y 0DZ
UK

www.summersdale.com

The authorized representative in the EEA is Hachette Ireland, 8 Castlecourt Centre, Dublin 15, D15 XTP3, Ireland (email: info@hbgi.ie)

Printed and bound in Poland

ISBN: 978-1-83799-561-5
eISBN: 978-1-83799-562-2

This FSC® label means that materials and other controlled sources used for the product have been responsibly sourced

MIX
Paper | Supporting responsible forestry
FSC® C018236

Substantial discounts on bulk quantities of Summersdale books are available to corporations, professional associations and other organizations. For details contact general enquiries: telephone: +44 (0) 1243 771107 or email: enquiries@summersdale.com.

CONTENTS

INTRODUCTION

"What have the Romans ever done for us?" asks Reg, the Judean activist character in *Monty Python's Life of Brian* (1979), after his comrades mention sanitation, medicine, education, wine, public order and plenty else. If we ask the same question today, 1,500 years after the fall of Rome, we will have a much longer list. From law to politics, language to belief, art to architecture, commerce to technology, the modern world continues to be shaped by arguably the greatest civilization that ever existed.

But how did Rome begin, develop and ultimately collapse? What made it the pre-eminent culture, society and empire of its day? Who were Rome's most influential personalities – and its rebels and outsiders? And what was daily life like for the citizens of Rome?

War, betrayal, duplicity, narcissism, farce, debauchery, doomed love – the story of ancient Rome is as eventful as any of its own myths and dramas, or as any novel or Netflix series of our own time. Read on to find out about **Julius Caesar**'s rise and fall, **Mark Antony**'s manoeuvrings and the impact of their mutual lover

Cleopatra and other important women within and without Rome.

Powerful as Rome became, it was challenged by invaders such as **Hannibal** and internal dissent led by **Spartacus**, among others. As perhaps the world's first "multicultural" empire, it promoted people of colour to the highest offices, such as the Berber governor **Quintus Lollius Urbicus**.

We will see how profoundly ancient Rome has shaped our modern societies, in fields of knowledge from engineering to medicine, but also in our attitudes towards government, politics, law, sexuality and faith. Some of these influences are well known already, but we'll also take a look at football, fast food, advertising, comedy and environmentalism to discover some of the lesser-known debts we owe to Rome.

AN INTRODUCTION
TO ANCIENT ROME

From its origins in the eighth century BCE
to the fall of its Western Empire in 476 CE,
Rome lasted an impressive 1,200 years and
comprised a landmass of 5 million square
kilometres at its height in the second century CE.
Though the origins of the Roman Kingdom are
shrouded in mystery, there is firmer evidence
for the civilization's later development.

Some historians argue that Rome lasted
longer than 476 CE, given that the Byzantine
Empire, alternatively called the Eastern
Roman Empire, survived until 1453 CE, when
it was conquered by the Ottoman Empire.

Let's look at this extraordinary society's
chronology in more detail.

ANCIENT ROME: A TIMELINE

THE ROMAN KINGDOM (754–509 BCE)

754 BCE – So legend has it, twin brothers **Romulus and Remus** depose **Amulius**, the corrupt and illegitimate ruler of the city of **Alba Longa** in what is now central Italy.

753 BCE – Romulus and Remus establish a new city on the **River Tiber** on the **Palatine Hill** in what is today western Italy. The city is named Rome after Romulus, who becomes its first king. To encourage economic and population growth, Romulus welcomes a diverse range of immigrants, including slaves and fugitives.

752 BCE – Romulus cements his reputation for ruthlessness by ordering the mass abduction and rape of local **Sabine women**. This is followed by the conquest of Caenina, a nearby town, and the establishment of Rome's first colonies.

715–640 BCE – During the reigns of **Numa Pompilius** and **Tullus Hostilius**, the Roman Kingdom annexes other neighbouring territories, including Alba Longa, and creates new guilds, customs, religious beliefs, a calendar system and its first **Senate House** (**Curia Hostilia**).

667 BCE – **Byzantium** (in modern-day Istanbul, Turkey) is colonized by Megarian Greeks.

640–616 BCE – The reign of **Ancus Marcius** signals a new period of piety, with the high priest of Rome (**pontifex maximus**) overseeing the transcription of religious rituals to wooden tablets for public consumption. Ancus Marcius achieves military victories over the Latins, Sabines and Veientes, and he builds new fortresses, ports and a bridge across the Tiber.

535 BCE – Although popular with Roman commoners for expanding the franchise, King **Servius Tullius** has become increasingly autocratic and arrogant by the time he is assassinated by his daughter Tullia and son-in-law **Lucius Tarquinius Superbus**.

509 BCE – Although scholars have challenged this traditional account as likely mythical or at least exaggerated, the Roman monarchy under Lucius Tarquinius Superbus (nicknamed "Tarquin the Proud") is overthrown by a group of elite **patrician** (aristocratic) families after the king's second son rapes the noblewoman **Lucretia**. Tarquin's troops are defeated at the **Battle of Silvia Arsia**. In place of the monarchy, a power-sharing republic is founded and run by two consuls elected annually, with support from the Senate and other groups.

THE ROMAN REPUBLIC (508–27 BCE)

508–504 BCE – As Rome defeats the Clusians and Sabines, the consul **Publius Valerius Publicola** devolves some powers to **quaestors** (public officials).

494 BCE – In the **secessio plebis** (withdrawal of the commoners), the **plebeian** lower class protests its oppression through debt and discrimination and abandons Rome. As a concession, the patricians allow plebeians to elect **tribunes** to represent their interests. This is the catalyst for the class-based **Conflict of the Orders** that will rage throughout the Republic era.

471–439 BCE – The Republic oscillates between liberalization and authoritarianism, with progressive measures such as the legalization of plebeian-patrician marriage offset by two periods of dictatorship led by **Cincinnatus**.

390 BCE – The **Senones of Gaul** (in modern-day France) sack Rome, destroying books and other valuable objects. Though archaeologists have since discovered that the Senones did little material damage to the city, the loss of cultural artefacts is partly why our knowledge of Roman history before this moment is hazy.

295 BCE – After defeats in the **Samnite Wars**, Rome wins the **Battle of Sentinum** against an alliance of Samnites, Etruscans and others.

280–272 BCE – Expanding into Greek-speaking lands, Rome takes on the superior armies of King **Pyrrhus**. After Pyrrhus wins big at **Heraclea and Asculum**, he is beaten decisively at **Tarentum**. Rome becomes the pre-eminent civilization of Italy. Pyrrhus is later killed in Greece when a woman hurls a tile at his head.

218–201 BCE – During the **Second Punic War**, **Hannibal**, a brilliant general of **Carthage** (in contemporary Tunisia), invades Italy with a force of men and elephants and comes close to conquering Rome.

146 BCE – Rome obtains its first territory in Africa after conquering Carthage after the **Third Punic War**.

91–88 BCE – Rome grants citizenship rights to its outlying subjects after the **Social War** uprisings.

15 MARCH 44 BCE – **Julius Caesar** is assassinated by senators appalled by his increasing autocracy.

43–30 BCE – The Republic disintegrates into civil war between factions led by **Octavian** and **Mark Antony**. Octavian overcomes Mark Antony and his ally and lover **Cleopatra VII**, bringing her **Kingdom of Egypt** under Roman control.

THE ROMAN EMPIRE (27 BCE–476 CE)

27 BCE – **Octavian** is coronated Emperor **Augustus**. Granted immense personal power, he initiates the **Pax Romana**, a time of relative peace, cohesion and expansion.

30–33 CE – **Jesus Christ** is reputedly crucified in the Roman colony of **Judea**, spawning a seminal new religion, **Christianity**.

64 CE – Under the megalomaniacal **Nero**, the **Great Fire of Rome** wrecks large parts of the city. Nero blames and persecutes Christians for starting the blaze.

66–70 CE – Inequality and injustice in Judea fuels the **Jewish Revolt**. The Romans destroy Jerusalem, massacring 500,000.

96–180 CE – The **Five Good Emperors** is a golden age of competent and ethical rulers, including **Hadrian** and **Marcus Aurelius**.

284–305 CE – After decades of social problems and attacks from foreign tribes, the empire is split by **Diocletian** into the **Tetrarchy** (four administrative sections) and then divided into the **Eastern** and **Western Roman Empires**.

379–395 CE – Under **Theodosius I**, Rome adopts Christianity as the state religion.

410 CE – The **Visigoths** sack Rome. This is the beginning of the end of the civilization.

476 CE – The Roman Empire collapses from external threats and internal turmoil.

VIOLENT ORIGINS

A great civilization often begets another great civilization, but not without bloodshed. Survivors of the Greek conquest of **Troy**, so the myth goes, fled with their prince **Aeneas** to North Africa, then on to **Latium** in what is now central Italy. The Roman historian **Livy** (59–17 BCE) claimed that Aeneas' son **Ascanius** founded the city of Alba Longa in Latium in around 1152 BCE. Ascanius was also said to be the ancestor of future patricians, including Julius Caesar.

After generations of stability, King Numitor was overthrown in the first of many power struggles that would come to define ancient Rome. His virgin daughter, **Rhea**, was raped and birthed twin boys, Romulus and Remus. Believing the father to be **Mars**, the god of war, Rhea abandoned her boys by the River Tiber to protect them. They survived by suckling on a wolf and were raised by herdsmen.

Romulus and Remus later restored Numitor to his throne and built a new city on the Palatine Hill. Romulus killed his brother in yet another contest for power. In 753 BCE, Romulus declared himself ruler and gave his name to the new kingdom.

A GRIM SOLUTION

Early Rome's population was low and needed to grow. Since women from neighbouring tribes looked down on Romans as socially inferior and refused to marry them, Romulus hit on a grim solution. He organized a festival in honour of either the gods **Neptune** or **Consus**, to which the nearby Sabine community was invited. After much eating, drinking and game-playing, upon a pre-arranged signal, Roman men kidnapped Sabine women, took them to their homes and forcibly married them.

Though the incident has since been dubbed "The Rape of the Sabine Women", some historians argue that the word "rape" in this context is rooted in the Latin word "raptio", meaning "abduction" rather than sexual violence. Either way, it is unlikely the women's experience was pleasant.

The Sabine men took their revenge later, almost defeating the Romans in battle. The twist in this legend – and perhaps a self-serving one from the Roman perspective – is that the Sabine women intervened to stop the fighting, as they were by this point happily integrated into Roman society.

THE VERSATILE KING

Reigning for 24 years in the seventh century BCE, Ancus Marcius is thought to have inaugurated several important Roman traditions and techniques. Devoutly religious, he laid the foundations for the **Temple of Jupiter**, in honour of the pre-eminent god of the Roman canon and introduced the sacred rituals that ensured Roman soldiers went into combat as just and honourable participants.

While peace-loving by nature, Marcius was a skilled general, extending the borders of Rome through the conquest of the Latin town of **Medullia** and the construction of a bridge over the Tiber, the **Pons Sublicius**, that was reputedly a feat of engineering: it was built without nails so that it could be rapidly dismantled if enemies tried to use it to advance on Rome.

Ancus Marcius is said to have had a dark sense of humour about law and order. He constructed Rome's first prison, the **Mamertine**, beside the **Forum Romana**, which was the centre of public life, so that the prisoners would have to look on in envy at the fun and freedom they had been deprived of.

THE LAST KING

The seventh and final king of Rome, Lucius Tarquinius (Tarquin) Superbus (meaning "The Arrogant" or "The Proud") (534–509 BCE), was the prototype of a darker type of Roman leader. He came to power by assassinating his predecessor **Servius Tullius**, with help from his wife – and Servius' daughter Tullia – and governed as a tyrant, refusing to hold elections and spurning the Senate, whose role was to advise the monarch.

Tarquin's character is revealed in a story about a priestess who tried to sell him nine books called the **Sibylline Prophecies**. Tarquin rejected her price, so the priestess burned three of the books and offered him the remaining number for the same sum of money. Tarquin again refused; the priestess destroyed three more. Only then did Tarquin realize their value – and foolishly paid the same amount for the last three books as he could have done for all nine.

More productively, Tarquin constructed the first sewage system in Rome, the **Cloaca Maxima**, and annexed nearby territory, including **Gabii**, by cunningly sending his son **Sextus Tarquinius** to pretend to ally with the city against Rome.

TRAGIC LUCRETIA AND THE KINGDOM'S END

Sextus Tarquinius became obsessed with **Lucretia**, a patrician woman of virtue and poise. When she rejected his advances, he raped her. Lucretia blamed herself and committed suicide.

Lucretia's corpse was paraded through Rome and provoked a successful uprising led by her husband **Collatinus** and his ally **Lucius Junius Brutus**. The Tarquin family were banished from the kingdom. Collatinus and Brutus became joint consuls of the new Roman Republic in 509 BCE, promising an end to autocracy and the devolution of power to officials.

The events above are not based on sources from the time of the Roman Kingdom because none have survived. The information comes from fictional narratives or histories composed long after the fact. What we know – or think we know – of Aeneas and the origins of Rome comes from the poem *Aeneid* by **Virgil**, and of the Tarquins from the *History of Rome* by **Livy**.

THE PLEBS PUSH BACK

Despite attempts to democratize Rome, by 495 CE, the plebeian (from where we get the slang word "pleb") underclass was menaced by discrimination, inequality and debt. To show their discontent, the plebeian citizens would stop work and withdraw from the city in protest, known as a **secessio plebis**.

In the first secessio plebis, the plebeians took to the streets to protest against debt and refused, en masse, to fight against invading **Volscians**. The consul Servilius promised that plebeians who enlisted would be exempt from their debts while serving with the army. But the plebeians were further alienated when the Republic tried to recruit them for other conflicts and granted greater rights to lenders. Numerous plebeians deserted Rome to live on **Mons Sacer (the Sacred Mountain)**.

In 493 BCE, the plebeians returned to Rome after the consuls agreed to their being represented by ten elected tribunes. Tribunes were licensed to defend plebeians who had been mistreated by patricians.

Later secessios campaigned against the abolition of the right to judicial appeal, the forced marriages and murders of women such as **Verginia** (465–449 BCE) and the prohibition of romantic relationships between plebeians and patricians.

NOT QUITE THE FALL OF ROME

Although romanticized by the Romans themselves – and later historians – as a catastrophe, we now know that the Sack of Rome in 390 BCE by the Senones of Gaul caused minor damage and actually helped Rome to progress.

Led by the chieftain **Brennus**, the Senones had begun migrating into northern Italy. Tensions with Rome came to a head at the **Battle of the Allia**, north of Rome. The Senones won decisively, but Rome had committed most of its troops to the battle, leaving the city undefended.

The Senones entered Rome unhindered and found senators going about their daily business. A Senone soldier goaded a senator by touching his beard, prompting the senator to strike the Senone with his staff. In retaliation, the Senones massacred all the senators. It's likely they would have gone on to capture Rome's **Citadel** were it not for the squawks of the city's geese that raised the alarm, warning of the invaders.

The Senones were persuaded to leave with a ransom of 1,000 pounds of gold. Rome had recovered, but it had learned lessons. Subsequently, new fortifications were built and the military reformed.

MILITARY MIGHT

The Sack of Rome initiated centuries of military innovation. What had been a relatively undisciplined army in the Kingdom era, riven with class conflict and dependent on the vast Greek **phalanx** formation that was ineffective on rough terrain, became in the age of the Republic a professional outfit based on **maniples**, groups of 120 men who could manoeuvre easily around the battlefield.

Specialist maniples included **velites**, who would agilely harass the enemy with light weaponry, cavalry, who were strong and swift on horseback, and **triarii**, the heavily armoured, spear-wielding veterans who were the last line of defence.

The **Marian Reforms** in 107 BCE created **cohorts** of 480 men, permitted landless citizens to enlist and required all soldiers to serve for 16–20 years with a land pension upon retirement, thereby cultivating expertise and loyalty.

To suit Rome's imperial ambitions, in around 27 BCE, Augustus founded the elite **praetorian guard**, tasked with protecting the emperor, and helped develop the **legion**, an adaptable and resilient force of 5–6,000 men recruited from the empire's multicultural populace who could fight in any climate or landscape.

Rome's navy was equally pioneering, inventing **triremes** and **quinqueremes** (boats having three and five rows of oars, respectively), and formidable battleships for conflicts such as the Punic Wars. On land and at sea, the Romans used state-of-the-art **ballistae** (giant crossbows) and torsion-driven **onagers** (catapults that launched rocks, fireballs and even dead animals).

Smaller Roman weapons were skilfully designed. The **pilum**, a 6–7-foot spear, would bend out of shape upon impact, making it impossible to throw back. The **gladius** was an 18–24-inch double-edged sword, capable of serious damage yet light and easily controlled. This, along with the **lorica segmentata**, a flexible yet protective suit of armour made from interlinked iron strips, became iconic of the famed **legionary** soldier. A **scutum** (rectangular shield) was used in the **testudo** formation, in which soldiers would link their shields to create a protective wall. The testudo helped win the Punic Wars, the **Battle of Actium** (31 BCE) and the **Siege of Jerusalem** (70 CE).

ROME'S NEMESIS

After Rome had beaten Carthage in Sicily, Corsica and other parts of the Mediterranean during the **First Punic War**, a young Carthaginian nobleman, Hannibal (247–181 or 183 BCE), promised his father "never to be a friend of Rome". In 218 BCE, now a general, Hannibal invaded **Saguntum** (in modern-day Spain), a Roman ally, triggering the **Second Punic War**.

In an epic journey, Hannibal's forces crossed the Alps into Italy. With an astonishing ability to predict his opponent's strategies and the deployment of war elephants to devastating effect, he defeated Rome at **Trebia** and **Lake Trasimene**. At the **Battle of Cannae**, he surrounded the Romans cunningly and annihilated 70–80,000 troops.

Hannibal lacked the resources to march directly on Rome and got bogged down in a war of attrition with the acclaimed general **Quintus Fabius Maximus**. Rome clawed back territory over the years and overcame Hannibal at the **Battle of Zama**, near Carthage, in 202 BCE. Refusing to forgive him for humiliating them, the Romans chased Hannibal to **Bithynia** (in modern Turkey). As troops encircled the house he was hiding in, Hannibal poisoned himself.

HAIL, CAESAR!

Arguably, no single figure is more important in Rome's transition from Republic to Empire than Julius Caesar (100–44 BCE). He is the best-known individual associated with ancient Rome, but not for positive reasons.

Belonging to a long-standing but uninfluential patrician family, the extremely ambitious Caesar was elected first as **pontifex maximus** (the highest priest in Rome) and eventually as consul, ruling in the **First Triumvirate** alongside **Pompey** (106–48 BCE) and **Crassus** (115–53 BCE). A gifted general, Caesar extended Rome's boundaries after ruthlessly repressing tribes in what are now Germany, France and Switzerland. At the **Siege of Alesia**, his troops defeated both the Gauls' standing army and their relief force. He also had successes in Egypt, Spain and Britain. Caesar recorded these campaigns in Roman literary masterpieces.

Caesar became a dictator, alienating public opinion. A narcissist, he was the first living Roman to have his face depicted on coins. On 15 March 44 BCE – since called the **Ides of March** – conspirators stabbed him 23 times as he sat on his golden throne in the Senate. As he died, Caesar reportedly said to **Brutus**, the lead conspirator, "You too, child?"

INFIGHTING TOWARDS AN EMPIRE

Before he was assassinated, Caesar had started a civil war with Pompey by crossing the Rubicon River and stating, "The die is cast." Despite Caesar beating Pompey at the **Battle of Pharsalus** in 48 BCE, rivalry between his loyalists and his enemies outlived him.

After Caesar's death, the **Second Triumvirate** was formed by **Octavian**, **Lepidus** and **Mark Antony**. After avenging Caesar's murderers, these men turned on each other, with Octavian declaring himself Caesar's rightful heir and Mark Antony allying with his lover **Cleopatra** of Egypt.

Rome's swelling social and economic problems convinced the patricians that more authoritarianism was needed. Plebeian farmers were furious about their land being confiscated by **latifundia** (huge estates) owned by the wealthy. A new class of urban paupers, the **proletarii**, protested about discrimination and having to compete for work with the influx of slaves, who were usually captives taken by Roman armies after their overseas conquests. Around 500,000 slaves arrived during Julius Caesar's reign alone.

WHO WAS SPARTACUS?

Rebellion in the troubled late Republic is epitomized by Spartacus' uprising, which happened in 73–71 BCE. Or did it? No contemporary sources mention it, and the first accounts were written a century later by the historians **Plutarch**, **Appian** and **Florus**.

These narratives claim that Spartacus was a Thracian-born mercenary who deserted the Roman army and was enslaved as a gladiator. Gladiators were forced to fight one another to the death for the public's entertainment. Spartacus and 70 others escaped from their gladiatorial training school with wagons full of weaponry and fled to **Mount Vesuvius**. This was the third and perhaps most successful major slave revolt in Rome's history.

An intelligent strategist, Spartacus created a guerrilla-style army of ex-slaves, raiding local towns and winning battles against the Romans in what became known as the **Third Servile War**. Although Spartacus was finally defeated by the emperor Pompey's legions at the **River Sele**, he inspired later radicals across the world, from the leader of the Haitian slave rebellion **Toussaint L'Ouverture** to **Karl Marx** and the German **Spartacus League** (1915–18 CE).

THE ENCHANTRESS OF THE NILE

Though not a Roman, no woman played such a dramatic part in Roman history as **Cleopatra VII Thea Philopator** (69–31 BCE). In a male-dominated ancient world, Cleopatra competed with the most charismatic, learned and politically savvy men.

Born into the **Ptolemaic** royal family, she was an academic child, mastering several languages. She was joint monarch of Egypt with her brother **Ptolemy XIV** until they fell out and he exiled her. Reputedly smuggling herself into Julius Caesar's quarters rolled in a carpet, she charmed him, and they became lovers. Caesar helped restore her to the Egyptian throne.

Cleopatra and Caesar had a child together, and she was living with him when he was assassinated. She then fell in love with Mark Antony and sided with him in his war with Octavian, which they lost. As Octavian's forces marched on Alexandria, Mark Antony fell on his sword, but he only wounded himself. He survived long enough to find Cleopatra and die in her arms. Grief-stricken, Cleopatra killed herself with, as legend has it, an asp's bite – more likely she ingested poison.

MOTHER OF THE COUNTRY

Octavian cemented his personal authority over Rome at Actium in 27 BCE and became Augustus, the first Roman emperor. His wife, **Livia Drusilla** (59 BCE–29 CE), was as ruthless a political operator as any male of the time.

She first married **Tiberius Claudius Nero** (82–33 BCE), a supporter of Mark Antony, with whom she had two sons. She was either forced or requested to divorce Nero and marry Augustus. Before their wedding, Livia dreamed that an eagle dropped a hen clutching an olive branch into her lap. She saw this as a portent of fertility and imperial might.

While Augustus frequently sought her advice on political affairs, Livia had her own agenda, allegedly orchestrating the murders of potential heirs to the throne, **Gaius** and **Lucius Caesar**. These and other manoeuvres paved the way for her son Tiberius to become emperor in 14 CE, to which Augustus may have been opposed. Tiberius was so dependent on Livia's guidance that she was nicknamed the **"Mother of the Country"**.

A GOLDEN AGE... SORT OF

In the Pax Romana, the 200-odd years following Augustus' reign, there was relative stability, prosperity, law and order in the empire. But it was hardly peaceful for the tribes victimized by Rome. These included the **Cantabrians** in Spain, **Pannonians** in the Balkans, Jews in the **Near East** and **Nabataeans** in Arabia.

However, once defeated, these tribes were granted **Latin Rights**, which protected their citizens from crime, gave them land and allowed them to participate in Roman politics. Outlying citizens felt a sense of belonging when permitted to trade with Rome, join its armies and partake in its holy rituals.

In Britannia, around 43 CE, some Roman soldiers challenged a Celtic bard to a poetry competition. The Romans' Latin verse impressed the crowd, but not as much as the bard's story about a Roman failing to ride a Britannic horse. A centurion responded by mocking his own colleagues' attempts to fish in local rivers. The crowd roared with laughter, and the Romans won the contest.

JEWS, CHRISTIANS AND RESISTANCE

Not everyone was keen to be incorporated into Rome. Soon after Pompey seized the great city of **Jerusalem** in 63 BCE and converted the region around it, Judea, into a Jewish-ruled dependency of Rome, there was a revolt against corruption, heavy taxation and religious discrimination. The **Zealots** were the most fiercely nationalist faction in Judea.

When King **Archelaus** died in 6 CE, Judea came under the direct control of the Roman governor **Pontius Pilate**, which caused further tensions. Although the lack of contemporary sources makes events uncertain, Jesus Christ likely lived in Pilate's time – and died on his orders, given that his new creed, Christianity, threatened both Roman and Jewish authority.

The **Jewish-Roman Wars** (66–135 CE) saw some of the highest death tolls in Roman military history; up to 1.4 million Jews and 350,000 Romans and their loyalists died. Between these conflicts the emperor Hadrian (76–138 CE) took a zero-tolerance attitude to Jewish identity, abolishing Judea in favour of the new **Syria Palaestina** colony and rebuilding Jerusalem as **Aelia Capitolina**, from which Jews were banned.

MEN OF LETTERS

Seldom are the three greatest writers produced by a civilization alive at the same time. **Virgil** (70–19 BCE), **Horace** (65–8 BCE) and **Ovid** (43 BCE–17/18 CE) were roughly contemporaries during the turbulent changeover from Republic to Empire, and they were also major public figures due to performances and recitations of their work. Much of what we know about Rome today is thanks to them.

Virgil came from humble beginnings, studied philosophy, rhetoric and the Greek poets, and had the affluent politician **Maecenas** (70–8 BCE) as his patron. After publishing *Eclogues* and *Georgics* – poetry concerned with work, rural life and the human experience – he was commissioned by Augustus to write the *Aeneid*, an epic poem recounting the Trojan Wars and the foundation of Rome. Virgil died before completing his masterpiece and apparently wanted it burned after his passing. Luckily for us, it was not.

Credited with the dictum **"carpe diem"** ("seize the day"), Horace penned lyric poetry both serious and amusing. The satirist **Persius** said of him, "As his friend laughs, Horace slyly puts his finger on his every fault; once let in, he plays about the heartstrings."

Unlike Virgil, who devoted himself exclusively to the writer's life, Horace was an adventurous soldier and politician, fighting in the Battle of Philippi in support of Brutus and the Republicans. In typical self-mocking fashion, he would later recount that he fled the battlefield like a coward without his shield. After being given amnesty by the Octavian regime, he became a vocal celebrant of it at this turbulent time in Roman affairs.

Ovid is best known for his ambitious and wide-ranging **Metamorphoses**, a hybrid of history and mythology in verse form that purports to tell the story of the world from its creation up until the time of Caesar. Though, like Virgil, he avoided politics, politics did not avoid Ovid – he was banished from Rome by Augustus for reasons unknown, the only clue we have is a cryptic comment he made about "a poem and a mistake". Historians have conjectured that the conservative emperor was offended by elements of Ovid's **Ars Amatoria** (**The Art of Love**), which discussed sexual and romantic relationships in detail.

THE WORST EMPEROR?

When determining the most egotistical and self-indulgent emperor of ancient Rome, there is stiff competition. Nero, who ruled from 54 to 68 CE, is up there, if accounts are to be believed.

Nero's banquets involved excessive consumption and baroque dishes such as flamingo tongues and stuffed peacocks. "Let us eat and drink, for tomorrow we die," he would say. He favoured elaborate hairstyles and expensive clothes, performed poetry and participated in chariot races despite having no talent in these fields.

While some sources claim he was popular among the lower classes, Nero was also violent and bigoted. He probably ordered the murders of his wife Claudia Octavia and his stepbrother Brittanicus. When the Great Fire of Rome struck in 64 CE – which some historians claim Nero caused to clear land on which to build his lavish Golden House palace – he scapegoated Christians and burned them alive.

Romans eventually lost patience with Nero. He fled the city when he learned that an army led by the governor of Hispania, **Servius Sulpicius Galba**, was marching to depose him. Nero stabbed himself to death before his enemies arrived.

KING OF COMEDY

After Nero's shambolic administration, Rome was subsumed by political chaos in 69 CE. Elite factions vied for power, and no fewer than four emperors reigned in just one year. The last of them, **Vespasian** (who served 69–79 CE), brought calm by instituting economic reforms and an ambitious construction programme. He had earned respect in his previous career as a **legate** (a high-ranking military officer), serving in the Roman conquest of Britain and helping to defeat the tribes of what is now the West Country in England.

As emperor, he was known for his mischievous sense of humour, which endeared him to people and differentiated him from other Roman leaders. When he introduced a tax on urine, which was bought and sold for tanning leather and other purposes, his son deemed the policy distasteful. Vespasian held up one of the coins that had been collected and retorted, "Money doesn't stink."

On his deathbed, Vespasian mocked the Roman custom of turning emperors into deities. "Oh dear, I think I am becoming god," he is supposed to have quipped.

MULTICULTURAL ROME

In 2017, a heated debate on social media discussed the historical accuracy of a modern cartoon depicting a multi-ethnic family in Roman Britain. However, there is much evidence that people of colour were not only integrated into the empire but rose to senior positions within it. While across Roman lands there were divisions on the bases of class, wealth, gender and faith, racism as we would define it today was not a particular factor.

The Roman military was one of the most diverse in history, recruiting men from across Africa and Western Asia.

Born in **Leptis Magna** (now Libya) in Roman-ruled Africa, **Septimus Severus** was emperor from 145–211 CE. He had Libyan-Punic and Roman ancestry. When Septimus visited the garrison at Hadrian's Wall, erected to deter raiders in the north of Britannia, an Ethiopian soldier offered him a garland as a sign of respect. There were also Syrians and Mauri from northwestern Africa stationed there.

DIVIDED, RULED AND PERSECUTED

By the time **Diocletian** came to power in 284 CE, Rome was in terminal crisis politically, socially and economically. Its bureaucracy and government, once efficient and disciplined, were beset by coups, civil wars and corruption. Hyperinflation and heavy taxation had wrecked the living standards of many citizens. The military was stretched to breaking point by incessant barbarian assaults along Rome's vast borders.

To solve these crises, Diocletian used his enormous personal authority to divide the empire into two administrative units: the East, containing Asia Minor, Egypt and the Levant; and the West, encompassing Italy, Gaul, Hispania and Britannia. He shared his power with three other newly created emperors and established four new administrative sub-capitals. To stabilize the new set-up, he eliminated threats to the empire from the **Sarmatians** (of modern Iran), **Carpi** (of modern Romania) and other tribes.

In spite of these reforms, internal conflicts and power struggles returned. Further discord was sown by Diocletian and his co-rulers initiating the **Great Persecution** (303–311 CE), the harshest victimization of Christians so far in Roman history.

It was precisely the burgeoning popularity of Christianity that prompted the emperors' merciless crackdown. Thousands were publicly fed to lions and wild boars in a punishment since made infamous in books and films about Rome. Others were beheaded or burned at the stake. Some survived by renouncing their faith after torture or imprisonment.

When **Constantine** (272–337 CE) came to power as ruler of the Western Empire in 306 CE, he resolved to re-unify Rome through a combination of military action and religious tolerance. He consolidated his power over both wings of the empire by defeating **Maxentius**, who controlled Italy and Africa, at the **Battle of the Milvian Bridge** (312 CE), and **Licinius**, emperor of the Eastern Empire, in 324 CE.

It is speculated that Constantine converted to Christianity just before his showdown with Maxentius after having a vision of the **Chi-Rho** symbol (☧), the Greek word for Christ. His **Edict of Milan** (313 CE) granted Christians the freedom to practise their beliefs.

A NEW CHRISTIAN CAPITAL

Given that the eastern zone of the empire had grown wealthier and more secure than the west, it made sense to Constantine to found a new capital city, which he named **Constantinople** (on the site of modern-day Istanbul, Turkey). Visitors to the city in its heyday were beguiled by its beauty and modernity.

Constantinople became a core of Christian worship, teaching and culture, reflected by the building of the **Church of the Holy Apostles**, eventually Constantine's burial place, and the **Church of the Holy Wisdom**, which evolved into the **Hagia Sophia**, still standing today although heavily reworked. With their beautiful arches and domes, these and other edifices influenced ecclesiastical architecture for many centuries. The pioneering use of brick and mortar was another triumph of Constantinople's built environment. In the fifth century CE, the emperor Theodosius erected the **Great Walls of Constantinople** comprising turrets, moats and two rows of robust fortifications.

Constantinople's position on the Bosporus Strait, between the Black Sea and the Mediterranean, allowed the Romans to dominate vital trade routes and made the city easily defendable against invaders from land and sea.

THE INEVITABLE FALL

The political, economic and religious reforms of the late imperial era extended Rome's life expectancy, but all great civilizations must come to an end. Historians have long argued about why Rome fell, but there are certain agreed facts.

As the tribes neighbouring Western Roman territory progressed socially and militarily, so they posed a greater menace. If the Eastern Empire had been rejuvenated by the shift of power, the West remained blighted by political infighting and economic deterioration. This was exploited by **Huns** (from the Central Asian Steppes), **Goths** (Scandinavia) and **Vandals** (central Europe), who frequently raided Roman lands.

These invasions culminated in the Sack of Rome (410 CE), masterminded by **King Alaric** of the **Visigoths**, who ran riot in the city for three days, looting, pillaging and razing property. Though there were only hundreds of casualties, the incident convinced many Romans that their empire was terminally weak and vulnerable.

The Western Empire withered away, barbarians moving in and occupying much of its space. The final straw came in 476 CE with a coup against the last emperor, Romulus Augustulus, led by the Germanic monarch Odoacer.

ROME 2.0?

After the Western Roman Empire collapsed, the Eastern Empire flourished and evolved into the Greek-speaking **Byzantine Empire**. It was so-called after Constantinople's name was changed back to Byzantium, the appellation of the Greek city formerly on its site. At its height in the mid-sixth century CE under the emperor **Justinian**, the Byzantine Empire encompassed about 1.3 million square kilometres, including its Anatolian heartlands, the Balkans, parts of North Africa and regions of Italy reconquered from the barbarians.

Throughout what in Europe is called the **Early Medieval** and **High Middle Ages**, the Byzantines were in many ways more advanced than any civilization in Europe. Compared to their neighbours, they were wealthier through trade and had sophisticated infrastructure, architecture, and legal and education systems. What would become the underpinnings of European culture – Christianity and classical Greek and Roman knowledge – was preserved and developed by the Byzantines before they exported it to the West.

Ultimately, the Byzantines went the way of the Western Romans, with political fragmentation and constant external attacks leading to the fall of Constantinople to the **Ottoman Empire** in 1453.

EVERYDAY LIFE

To the modern observer, everyday life in ancient
Rome was a curious mix of attitudes, customs
and activities that are at once familiar, since
we inherited many of them, and shockingly
different. Certain Roman approaches to justice,
governance, urban planning and leisure have
strongly shaped our own, whereas sacrifices,
public executions, exploitation and religious
persecution strike most of us today as outlandish.

In this chapter, we'll explore what it was like to be
an ordinary Roman citizen: how you ate, drank,
dressed, studied, worked, formed relationships,
raised children and amused yourself.

THE EMPIRE EATS

As Roman power broadened, so did the variety of foods available from the newly acquired provinces. Most people consumed three meals a day. The **ientaculum** (breakfast) was little more than bread and water or **vinum** (wine) for the commoners, while the better-off enjoyed olives, dates, figs and cheese. Around noon, **cena** could feature **puls** (grain porridge), beans, chickpeas and, if you were lucky, salted or cured meat. The **vesperna** was an evening tea similar to the ientaculum.

The upper classes would have **prandium** (light lunch) at noon before an often long and lavish cena, which included different courses of meat, fish, fruit and veg. Romans loved wine, sometimes with added honey or herbs, and children drank **lac** (milk). **Cervisia** (beer) was seen as a lower-order or barbarian beverage.

Spiced and pork-stuffed **gliridae** (dormice), seasoned sow's womb, giraffe and boiled ostrich were Roman favourites. The sweet-savoury divide was crossed by honey-glazed grasshoppers and fish mixed with fruit.

SIMPLE BUT PRACTICAL DRESS

Given the warm weather, Romans tended to wear variations of tunics – sleeved for females, short-sleeved or sleeveless for males. For special occasions men and boys donned the **toga**, a semi-circular piece of woollen cloth, while women and girls preferred the cloak-like **palla** over a **stola** (long, baggy dress). Sandals and slippers were common footwear in cities, clogs sometimes in the countryside.

The **paenula** (thick, hooded leather or woollen cape) gave warmth and protection from inclement weather. Women got married in a veil called the **flammeum**, coloured orange or scarlet to represent passion and fertility.

Religion intersected with fashion in the form of the **bulla**, an attractive amulet worn to ward away malevolent spirits.

> Emperors and victorious generals were allowed to wear the **toga picta**, a purple toga with elaborate gold embroidery, and the **tunica palmata**, a tunic adorned with palm leaves.

CLASS FACTS

The Roman class system was based on wealth, work, land ownership and political rights. Atop the hierarchy were the patricians of the oldest dynasties. They were often major landlords and occupied senior positions in government, bureaucracy, the military and the priesthood.

Enjoying social and political clout, the **senatorial class** were qualified to stand for the Senate if they possessed land and wealth.

Originating in the ranks of the cavalry, the **equestrian** middle class were traders, tax collectors and moneylenders. Equestrians could attain riches and prestige without having been born into noble families.

The plebeians were the working-class majority, including farmers, labourers and small businesspeople. They couldn't stand for political office, suffered legal discrimination and were expected to be the foot soldiers in Rome's wars. When Rome urbanized in the imperial epoch, an even less privileged stratum called the proletarii emerged.

Liberti were former slaves with even fewer rights than the plebeians. **Servi** (slaves) were treated as sub-human and could be bought and sold as property. They were forced to do unpaid menial work.

A HARSH REALITY

Slavery was a vital component of Roman society from the fifth century BCE. If you were a slave in the countryside, you would be forced to work in agriculture or mining. In the cities you would have to cook and clean for – even educate and entertain – patrician families. You were subject to abuse and beatings. Your only chance of a career change was if you were sold on to another owner.

Rome's imperial growth massively increased the population of captured and enslaved foreigners. It was not impossible to free yourself as a slave. If your master was kind, they could legally **manumit** (release) you, or you could somehow find the money to buy your liberty from them. Other slaves escaped to freedom but had to live as fugitives.

Unlike the later **Atlantic Slave Trade**, Roman bondage had little to do with race and ethnicity other than certain nationalities being given particular duties. Barbarians were preferred for manual labour, while women from Judea, Britannia, Greece and elsewhere were enslaved in **lupinaria** (brothels).

EARNING A LIVING

Since 70–90 per cent of Romans lived in rural regions, the most common work was farming. **Coloni** (tenant farmers) rented plots from estate owners in return for cash or a portion of their produce. They were vulnerable to debt and bad harvests. **Smallholders** were better off due to owning their land, feeding themselves from it and selling any surplus at the market.

Slaves and proletarii were limited to agricultural labour, building, acting, dancing, baking and street-food vending. While today we think of medicine as a middle-class profession, Roman current and former slaves in Rome could be **physicians**.

Recognizing the precarity of workers, the Roman state introduced the **annona** (dole handouts) in the third century BCE, and the programme was later expanded by Julius Caesar and Augustus. At times of scarcity the poor would be given grain with which to make bread and other foods. This likely prevented mass starvation at certain junctures in Rome's history.

POWER AND (UN)ACCOUNTABILITY

A citizen's rights and freedoms were determined by a political system based on Greek philosopher **Plato**'s (427–348 BCE) thoughts about republican governance. The Republic ("**res publica**" in Latin means "affairs of state") aimed to distribute power beyond a single leader.

It was far from democratic. Adult male citizens could vote for the two consuls who ran Rome in the Republic era, but an **electoral college** (in which some blocks of votes carried more weight than others) allowed the elites to outvote the poor. The next rank was the **praetor**, who could judge legal cases and govern provinces. **Censors** were well-respected for counting citizens and property for tax gathering. Like these offices, members of the Senate advisory body were not elected but chosen from high-born officials. There was more accountability nearer the beginning of the **cursus honorum**, the journey a politician took to professional glory.

The plebeians' aspirations were limited to becoming **aediles**, responsible for public works, policing and organizing games, and later, tribunes, who could veto policies if thought harmful to plebeians.

In the imperial age, emperors would frequently assume the role of **dictator**, taking all the power for themselves.

A WOMAN'S LOT

While women were second-class citizens in Rome under **patria potestas** (the control of men) they were highly respected for **maternitas** (motherhood) and could exercise considerable influence over the men in their lives. **Cornelia** (190–100 BCE) and **Agrippina the Younger** (15–59 CE) helped shape policy and even conspired to murder political adversaries.

While women could inherit land and wealth, they could not vote, take public office or join the military. Widows or women who had lost their male guardians had more liberty to manage their finances. Better-off females controlled their households, hiring staff, buying in provisions and conducting religious rites.

Against the grain of wider Roman inequality, women could easily obtain a divorce. The Roman author **Apuleius** tells the – possibly fictional – story of **Sulpicia**, who fell out of love with her husband and persuaded him that she was turning invisible from a curse. When she said she was worried about disappearing completely, her husband agreed to a divorce.

GIRL POWER BEHIND THE THRONE

Born into the prestigious Julio-Claudian dynasty, Agrippina the Younger might have given hope to Roman women unhappy with their social lot. Transcending the expectations of women in the early Republic, she was both a loving mother and a smart, feared political operator.

Agrippina married her uncle, the emperor **Claudius** (who reigned 41–54 CE) – which was not uncommon at the time – and is credited with bolstering his authority by ordering the deaths of rivals, including **Marcus Junius Silanus**. Her extraordinary knowledge of current affairs meant Claudius took her advice seriously when making appointments and devising policy. Though she initially preferred Claudius' son Britannicus as his heir, she manoeuvred behind the scenes to install her son, Nero, to the throne.

Nero came to resent his mother's meddling, and their relationship disintegrated after Claudius' death in 54 CE. Nero came to see her as a threat and organized her passage on a ship that he deliberately sank. She survived the shipwreck and escaped to her villa. Nero sent assassins to kill her in her bedroom.

EDUCATED TO SERVE ROME

Education was a privilege enjoyed by boys from rich families, though some girls received limited home instruction. Slaves and plebeians were usually illiterate and were only taught the basics needed for their jobs. Wealthier parents imparted moral values and practical skills until the age of seven when boys were sent to **ludus**, a primary school where they learned reading, writing and arithmetic using **tabulae** (wax tablets) and a stylus.

Aged 12, patrician boys attended **grammaticus** (secondary school) to learn Greek and Roman literature, language and philosophy. Greek intellectual culture was regarded as the precursor to Rome's and was highly regarded. These youths were taught works by **Homer**, **Virgil**, **Cicero** and **Terence**. At 16, boys received the **rhetorical training** necessary for their future work as lawyers, politicians or bureaucrats. They were tutored by a **rhetor** (specialist in oratory and debate).

In addition, fathers were expected to share with their sons knowledge of military strategy, farming and civic duties. Girls' home education equipped them to be housewives. They learned to read, write and add up enough to be able to later manage their household.

THE GREAT DEBATER

Perhaps the most acclaimed rhetor of ancient Rome was **Cicero** (106–43 BCE). A Renaissance Man before the term existed, he was a gifted statesman, lawyer, writer and philosopher, today known for his pearls of wisdom such as "Freedom is participation in power" and "The safety of the people shall be the highest law."

Though his political accomplishments included thwarting the **Catiline** coup (63 BCE) against the consuls by catching and executing its ringleaders, he is best remembered for his debating abilities and scholarship. He frequently shifted public opinion with his passionate and persuasive speeches and contributed hugely to the development of the Latin language by coining many new words and phrases.

Cicero became a role model for young, ambitious Roman men eager to make a name for themselves in government, law and the military. Most of his writings survived and have inspired **John Milton**, **Thomas Jefferson**, **Martin Luther King Jr** and **Barack Obama**, who has admitted to drawing on Cicero's style for his own political speeches.

KEEPING IT CLEAN

One of the more egalitarian aspects of Rome was its public bathhouses, which were open to rich and poor, even if some had exclusive areas reserved for the elites. Baths fell into two categories: **thermae** (large complexes that could also feature libraries, taverns and gardens) and **balnae** (smaller affairs that could be public or private).

Essential both to hygiene and socialization, baths contained a **palaestra** (gymnasiums where patrons exercised before bathing), **tepidarium** (a warmed room that helped customers acclimatize), **caldarium** (a kind of sauna) and **frigidarium** (a cold chamber or pool). Before washing, Romans covered their bodies in olive oil and scraped off the dirt with a tool called a **strigil**. Roman baths showcased engineering prowess, with a circulation of hot air under the floors and a supply of water through aqueducts.

Famous bathhouses included the beautifully decorated **Baths of Caracalla** (completed 217 CE) and the **Baths of Diocletian** (306 CE), the largest complex in ancient Rome and able to hold 3,000 people at once.

ROMAN RELIGION

The Romans were **polytheists**, revering a pantheon of deities whom they believed influenced almost every area of life: war, politics, work, love, family and health.

Roman gods and goddesses were closely modelled on their Greek counterparts, a result of early encounters with Greek culture and beliefs during Rome's acquisitions of parts of the eastern Mediterranean. Both cultures placed great importance on **omens**, signs in nature that the gods were acting in one way or another.

The highest deity in Roman mythology was **Jupiter**, the chief of the gods, associated with thunder and lightning, with great similarities to the Greek **Zeus**. So the legend goes, he was born to **Saturn**, the god of time and agriculture, and **Ops**, associated with fertility and abundance. Saturn was afraid that his son would usurp him so he set out to swallow him. To save Jupiter, Ops tricked Saturn by wrapping a rock in swaddling clothes. She hid Jupiter on Mount Ida, where he was nurtured by nymphs (spirits representing natural features like lakes and mountains) until he grew strong enough to overthrow Saturn.

Jupiter's wife **Juno** was the goddess of marriage and childbirth. Other major deities included **Mars** (the god of war), **Venus** (love and beauty), **Minerva** (wisdom) and **Neptune** (the ocean). Each Roman deity had a particular personality, skills and attributes, and temples were built in their honour throughout the Roman Empire. Lesser figures in the pantheon included **Laverna**, goddess of thieves, **Mefitis**, goddess of noxious fumes, and **Vertumnus**, god of seasons.

Roman mythology was filled with legends that explained the births of the gods, heroic adventures and the origins of the world. These tales often borrowed elements from Greek mythology, adapting them to suit Roman morality and values. The Greek myth of the **Twelve Labours of Heracles** was adapted by the writer **Seneca** (4–65 CE) to symbolize Roman virtues of courage, honour, fortitude and **stoicism**.

As Rome's borders widened, it absorbed countless spiritual practices and ideas from conquered peoples, leading to a **syncretism** of beliefs (see pages 93–4). This could be both a binding force and the cause of tension.

RELIGION AND EVERYDAY LIFE

Wherever you were in the Roman social hierarchy, you would participate in rituals, festivals and sacrifices. Family homes featured a **lararium**, a shrine in honour of the **Penates** (gods of the pantry) and **Lares** (household deities). It was believed that misfortune would strike the home and all those in it if offerings of food, wine and incense were not made.

For blessings and spiritual protection, Romans could visit temples and public altars to consult priests and priestesses, who were seen as conduits to the gods' favour. Priests, known as **flamines** and **augurs**, were part of the elite and would preside over public ceremonies and festivals.

The **Vestal Virgins** were priestesses dedicated to the goddess Vesta, who looked after the hearth and home. They were tasked with tending the sacred fire in the **Temple of Vesta**, which ensured Rome's security and prosperity. Highly respected in Roman society, a Vestal Virgin was usually recruited at six or ten years of age and had to remain chaste for 30 years.

THE CHRISTIAN LIFE

Christianity, which spread west from Judea after the death of Jesus Christ in the first century CE, radically changed the lives of ordinary Romans and had profound social impacts. At first, Christianity was severely repressed, not least because it was monotheistic (belief in one god) rather than polytheistic (belief in many gods) and regarded as foreign and subversive.

Early Christians had to share their creed and conduct rituals like the Eucharist (representing Jesus' Last Supper) secretively in their homes and at private gatherings. Being found out could result in execution and **martyrdom** if they refused to recant their beliefs.

But the Christian message of love, equality, empathy and humility caught on, especially among the poorer and marginalized sections of Roman society, who were alienated from the existing values of power, honour and accepting one's place in the social order.

Life got infinitely better for Roman Christians after the Edict of Milan in 313 CE, which legalized the faith and helped it to reach many new converts.

HEALTH AND WELLBEING

The average life expectancy in ancient Rome was 20–30 years of age, a third less than in developed nations today. Most people were deprived, lived in unhygienic conditions and had little healthcare beyond herbal treatments. Diseases like smallpox, measles and the plague were common, with the **Antonine Plague** (165–180 CE) killing over 5 million people and the **Cyprian Plague** (249–262 CE) leading to social breakdown and religious panic.

That said, the invention and evolution of aqueducts and sewage systems improved hygiene, and most Romans bathed regularly, which staved off illness. There was a devotion to physical fitness, and wrestling, running and swimming were all popular pastimes. And the Roman diet tended to be balanced and nutritious, comprising fruits, grains, vegetables and meat.

It is believed that the emperor **Caligula** liked to bathe in a mixture of crocodile bile and honey. While he sat back and enjoyed his bath, certain that it was good for his health, his court members would vomit from the stench.

COMPETENCE, CURES AND CURSES

Roman doctors amassed knowledge about surgery, drugs, wound treatment and rehabilitation from other cultures such as Greece and Egypt, and they made their own advances in these fields. These were particularly evident in **valetudinaria** (military hospitals) containing outpatient departments, recovery spaces and surgical theatres. Patricians often employed a private doctor and had small-scale healthcare facilities in their homes.

Born in Pergamon near the Aegean Sea, **Galen** (129–between 200 and 216 CE) settled in Rome, where he became arguably that society's greatest doctor. While working as a private physician to several emperors, including Marcus Aurelius, Galen recorded in great detail his discoveries in physiology, anatomy and pharmacology. He proposed an early and fairly accurate explanation of blood circulation and deduced that the brain controlled the body via the nervous system. His most famous theory is that of the **four bodily humours**:

phlegm, blood, black bile and yellow bile, which he believed were key to understanding human health.

Roman medical care had many defects that ordinary citizens could fall foul of, if not careful. The intertwining of superstition with medicine cost many lives, with people often preferring to trust in the power of a charm or a priest's blessing over the **scientific method**, which was in its infancy.

Galen's insights into the anatomy of animals did not always translate to the human body. Misapplied techniques such as **bloodletting** could weaken or kill patients, as we know all too well today. **Mercury** and **lead** were swallowed or applied to wounds, which would instead poison patients.

Like us, the Romans used **opium** as an efficient painkiller, but, unlike us, they were unaware of its considerable addictiveness. Though remarked upon for the "warm feeling" it gave users, **cannabis** was frowned upon for supposedly leading to headaches, nausea and impotence.

ALL IN THE HEAD

Galen seems to have had a progressive attitude to **mental health**, writing, "It may be that under certain circumstances 'thinking' is one of the causes that bring about health or disease because people who get angry about everything and become confused, distressed and frightened for the slightest reason often fall ill for this reason and have a hard time getting over these illnesses."

But mental healthcare in Rome was primitive, with very disturbed patients held in confinement in the misguided hope that they would recover that way. Romans knew and wrote about disorders such as insomnia, lethargy, agitation, phobias and melancholia, which today we call depression. These problems were thought to be caused by supernatural forces, personal moral shortcomings or lack of individual competence.

There was a trust in cures both evidence-based and not so much: prayers and rituals, herbs such as **mugwort** and **valerian**, abstention from wine, improved diet, music and art therapy, and learning the life lessons of philosophy.

HOME, NOT ALWAYS SWEET HOME

Most poor families in Rome's urban areas lived in **insulae**, unhygienic multistorey apartment buildings. In a sense, they are the predecessors of our modern **tower block** and **high-rise** structures. On higher floors, the quarters were plusher and larger, with cramped and less pleasant dwellings nearer the ground. As with many contemporary tower blocks, ground-floor units were often stores or other businesses.

Insulae were made of brick or concrete, supported by wooden beams. Typically, each apartment would comprise a lounge, sleeping area and a space in which to cook. Drinking water and bathing facilities were usually communal, located at the foot of the building or shared among several blocks.

The minority of well-heeled Roman families dwelled in a **domus**, a large house with columns and sophisticated marble panelling and decorations. Many had atriums, private gardens and numerous rooms for entertaining guests and accommodating slaves and servants.

The wealthiest patricians would, in addition to their domus, own large **villas**. **Villa rusticae** were country homes, usually attached to an estate or farm, while **villa urbanae** were based in cities.

THE GREAT ENGINEER

Guided by three fundamental principles – **firmitas** (strength), **utilitas** (utility) and **venustas** (beauty) – **Vitruvius** was perhaps Rome's most famous engineer, though little is known about his life. He lived in the first century BCE and worked as an architect, engineer, soldier and author.

His innovations in the design of arches, aqueducts, mechanical systems and town planning made life more comfortable and less dangerous for many ordinary Romans. It is possible he was recruited into Julius Caesar's army, where he specialized in designing artillery machines such as the ballistae (pages 20–21).

Vitruvius published his thoughts and findings in ***De Architectura***, arguably the first significant work of engineering and architectural scholarship. In it he wrote, "He who is theoretic as well as practical, is therefore doubly armed; able not only to prove the propriety of his design, but equally so to carry it into execution."

The book's commentaries on civic engineering, temple design, pavement building, geometry, measurement and water supply were the inspiration for **Leonardo da Vinci**'s iconic *Vitruvian Man* drawing.

THE LAWS OF THE LAND

The Roman legal system was the most sophisticated of any civilization up to that point in history. It affected everyday life as intimately as religion did, shaping the citizens' rights and freedoms in areas from marriage to work, property to trade.

The **Twelve Tables**, established in 450 BCE, provided citizens protections relating to crime, property disputes and personal injury. While the law was originally stacked in favour of the privileged, the plebeians achieved greater rights through protest and their representation by tribunes.

Roman courts settled both civil and criminal cases, contested by lawyers and adjudged by magistrates. They could be rowdy affairs with the public allowed to heckle. In theory, every Roman, rich or poor, could access courts, but the better-off and the better-connected tended to win disputes and trials.

The success of Roman commerce is ascribed to tight regulation and strict contracts, which helped small businesspeople and farmers to prosper. More oppressively, patria potestas gave absolute legal power to the male head of a household, rendering his wife and children second-class citizens, comparatively.

CRIME AND PUNISHMENT

Fines and lashings were the most common punishments for petty crimes like theft. Major misdemeanours like murder and rebelling against your slave master could result in crucifixion. Perhaps even more unpleasant was **poena cullei**, wherein the felon was sealed in a sack alongside snakes, dogs or monkeys before being thrown into a river. This grisly fate was for those found guilty of **parricide** (killing a parent).

Damnatio ad bestias, or being thrown to wild animals in the arena, was a form of public execution used for serious crimes, often involving Christians or rebellious slaves. The spectacle of seeing a person torn apart by animals was intended to serve as both punishment and entertainment.

You could be landed with a heavy fine if you committed **ostentatio cadaveris** (displaying a corpse incorrectly) or cut down someone else's trees without permission. In such a religious society that respected its great ancestors, just about the worst crime you could be guilty of was grave robbing, the penalty for which was death.

THE BOTTOM LINE

The Roman economy was generally robust thanks to a well-structured currency system tied to a productive agricultural sector. The main coins were **denarius** (silver), **sestertius** (bronze or brass) and **aureus** (gold). Lower denominations included **as** and **quadrans**. The currency could be spent all over the empire, which facilitated trade and investment.

The extensive network of Roman roads and sea routes (especially in the Mediterranean) was good for business too, enabling the importation and exportation of essential and luxury goods to wider Europe, Asia and Africa.

Rome blazed many trails in banking and finance, with credit available to develop businesses, and currency exchange services making life easier for travelling merchants. **Argentarii** (bankers) and others engaged in commerce were legally obligated to operate fairly and ethically, though cheating and corruption were not unheard of.

Roman trading was more professionalized than it had ever been in history, with codified laws and **collegia** (guilds) protecting the interests of merchants and craftspeople. Well-off Romans made long-term investments in slaves, land and business ventures.

TRICKS OF THE TRADE

Romans would buy or sell their wares at markets of different shapes and sizes, depending on where they lived. Village markets were loud and colourful events, where artisans, merchants and craftspeople vended food, drink, pottery and textiles. Town and city markets were even bigger and more vibrant, selling goods from all over the empire: amber from the **Baltic Sea**, olive oil from Iberia, ivory from Africa, metals from Britain and pearls from the Persian Gulf.

The economy periodically faltered due to war, outbreaks of disease, political friction and, later in Rome's story, barbarian invasion. Inflation was a regular scourge, especially when the government debased the currency by reducing the proportion of precious metals in its coins.

When the emperor **Tiberius** (reign 14–37 CE) reduced the Roman money supply and demanded the early recalls of loans, a financial crisis decimated businesses and crashed real estate prices. The crisis was fixed with the prompt and widespread granting of interest-free loans.

DOWNTIME, ROMAN-STYLE

Normally based in cities or along lengthy roads, **tabernae** and **cauponae** (taverns and inns) were happening hives of social activity. Romans of various backgrounds would drink wine, eat hearty stews, talk business, tell each other jokes and chatter late into the night. In addition, cauponae offered simple lodgings for travellers.

Looked down upon by the upper classes, the **popina** was a rowdier hangout, focusing more on drinking, gambling and prostitution. The intellectuals Seneca and Cicero warned of the moral bankruptcy of popina life. During his reign, the emperor Augustus tried to crack down on the growing number of these venues.

The very privileged would not usually frequent popinae. But the story is told of a Roman senator, keen to be a man of the people, who disguised himself as a plebeian and went into his local popina. However, his upper-class accent and good manners gave him away as a patrician and the other patrons mocked him. The senator beat a hasty retreat, embarrassed.

LOVE AND MARRIAGE

Marriage was an important social institution in Rome, with sex between husband and wife intended primarily to produce heirs. Commonly married off at 13 or 14 years old, women had to be faithful to their husbands while men were allowed to have discreet liaisons with concubines, sex workers and slaves. Since slaves had no rights, they were vulnerable to abuse and exploitation.

The **Lex Julia** law of 18 BCE reflected this hypocrisy, with convicted female adulterers exiled, and their husbands penalized if they *did not* divorce them.

Roman marriages were usually arranged by parents whose main consideration was the status of potential spouses. Marriage was a legal matter involving a contract and a **dowry** (bride price). After a formal **sponsalia** (betrothal), a young couple could go on dates to forums, plays and festivals. Gifts would be exchanged, while poetry and humour were methods of flirting.

Children born out of wedlock were often abandoned on rubbish heaps. "The boundary between contraception and infanticide was a blurred one," writes historian Mary Beard, "and disposing of children after birth was safer than getting rid of them before."

LGBTQ+ ROME

It was acceptable for Roman men, especially from the upper echelons, to have sexual relations with both males and females, as long as they played the dominant role. We know from the poetry of **Catullus** (84–54 BCE) and **Martial** (38–41 CE–102–104 CE), that male same-sex love was not only tolerated but appreciated. The only law relating to homosexuality was the **Lex Scantinia** (introduced in the second or third century BCE), which punished passive gay men, especially if they were plebeians or current or former slaves.

We know less about same-sex relationships between Roman women, but both Martial and the satirist **Juvenal** (55–138 CE) mention them briefly – and negatively – in their writings. There was arguably a gender-fluid aspect to **Galli** priests, men who would castrate themselves and take on feminine attributes. The Galli worshipped **Cybele**, a mother deity, and were marginalized by polite Roman society. The young emperor **Elagabalus** wore women's make-up and clothing, demanded to be called "my lady" rather than "my lord" and looked into having surgery that would give him female genitals.

DOOMED LOVE

Perhaps Rome's most notable gay man was the emperor Hadrian, who had a passionate yet ultimately tragic romantic relationship with **Antinous** (*c*.111–130 CE), a handsome young Greek from **Bithynia** (in present-day Turkey) about 35 years Hadrian's junior. Their bond is seen as the epitome of classical **pederasty** (a social and educational relationship between an older and younger male). Hadrian and Antinous' epic romance was widely recorded and admired by Roman historians, including **Cassius Dio**.

Antinous was Hadrian's travel companion on his exhaustive tours of the empire, including to Egypt and Athens. Antinous was only about 20 years old when he died suddenly, possibly by drowning in the River Nile. Hadrian was devastated, "the first to weep over him and to have made his grief manifest", as Cassius puts it.

There was a period of public mourning, Antinous apparently popular among ordinary Romans. Hadrian commemorated his late lover by founding the city of **Antinopolis** in Egypt and building a temple in his honour. Antinous was eventually deified.

POMPEII: INSIGHTS FROM DISASTER

In 79 CE, **Mount Vesuvius** erupted, burying the Roman city of **Pompeii** under volcanic ash and pumice. The historian **Pliny the Younger** (61–113 CE) described the start of the eruption thus: "A cloud... was rising from a mountain [it was afterwards known to be Vesuvius] whose form I cannot give you a more exact description of than by likening it to that of a pine tree. It rose to a great height on a sort of trunk and then split off into branches."

While this was clearly a catastrophe for the inhabitants at the time, archaeologists learned a great deal about daily life in Rome from the well-preserved buildings, mosaics, frescoes and other items. They also gained a good understanding of the layout of streets and structures of buildings.

Archaeologists in the eighteenth and nineteenth centuries CE excavated the remains of around 1,500 victims, deducing their final moments – and could even see the expressions on their faces – by taking plaster casts from the ash. Pompeii was made a **UNESCO World Heritage Site** in 1997 and is well worth a visit.

ART AND
CULTURE

Ancient Rome synthesized cultural traditions and artistic techniques taken from other civilizations it annexed and those that came before it. The result was an extraordinary range of forms, styles and practices – from architecture to literature, philosophy to sport, festivals to theatre – that continue to impress today.

If there was cruelty in gladiatorial combat and Roman stereotypes of conquered tribes, then there could be magnanimity in the ways Romans learned about spirituality from foreign peoples. Good and bad, it all makes for an eye-opening story.

MASTERS OF THE ARTS

Ancient Roman art made many innovations, including its realist depictions of the world and its creative representations of history and mythology. Sculpture included lifelike busts of prominent men and women, capturing fine details. The relief sculptures produced by moulding or sculpting features on buildings like **Trajan's Column** tell visual stories of crucial events in the civilization's history.

Used both for practical and decorative purposes, **terra sigillata** was a unique red pottery with a glossy finish and complex design. Mosaics were tessellations of small tiles or stones and can be found on the walls and floors of villas, temples and other public edifices. They were often status symbols, denoting the owner's prosperity and good taste.

Frescoes were a characteristic art form of ancient Rome, and many were found intact at Pompeii (page 71). Frescoes could represent gods and myths, but in Pompeii, they also depicted the surrounding rural landscape and rituals conducted by an enigmatic cult.

REAL AND IDEAL

Roman painting had its halcyon days between the first century BCE and the fourth century CE, taking ancient Greek art's preoccupations with idealism and realism in new directions. Public and private buildings were beautified with frescoes – arresting pictures made from applying pigments to plaster walls – which were particularly popular in the late Republic/early Empire phase. They told stories not only of gods and mythical heroes but also of ordinary people who worked in the fields, the streets and the home.

Roman portraiture was a mixture of **verism**, a style that brought out fine facial details to convey age and wisdom, and **idealization**, in which notable people such as emperors would be represented as young or godlike. The deep attention to detail also characterizes Roman **still life** painting.

The Romans broke the mould with the bedazzling **trompe-l'œil** technique, which produces optical illusions such as walls seeming to stretch into gaps and open spaces. A striking example of trompe-l'œil is in the **House of the Fruit Orchard** in Pompeii, where the walls were illustrated with trellises covered in birds and fruit, clouding the division between the indoors and outdoors.

SPECTACULAR STRUCTURES

Roman brilliance in engineering, aesthetics and grandeur is embodied in its architecture. Rome excelled at pillars, arches, domes and porticos (covered entrances) such as those of the Forum, the **Pantheon** (erected 27–25 BCE), the major temple, and the **Basilica Maximus**, a civic hall built between 308 and 312 CE.

Everything Romans understood about engineering, hydraulics and water management went into aqueducts like the **Pont du Gard**, established in the south of what is now France in 40–60 CE to supply water to the nearby town of **Nemausus** (modern-day Nîmes). Its three-tiered arch design has since become iconic.

Probably the most spectacular structures were the amphitheatres. The **Colosseum** could accommodate 50–80,000 people at once to watch athletics, gladiatorial games, **naumachiae** (mock sea battles) and theatrical productions. The building was remarkable for its **retractable awnings** and network of subterranean passages used by performers – both human and animal.

Other notable feats of Roman architecture include the **Ara Pacis** and its delightful reliefs relating to Pax, the goddess of peace, and the **Circus Maximus**, which could hold a whopping 250,000 spectators in its prime.

TRAJAN'S MARKET

Established by the emperor **Trajan** (98–117 CE) and excavated in the 1920s and 1930s, this complex has been partially restored and tells us much about Roman architecture and culture. Constructed across three levels on the terraced hillside, the market's ground level consists of shallow alcoves that once served as small shops and were originally framed with **travertine** (sedimentary rock).

The main building on the next level was an apartment block with a covered shopping arcade to its left. In front of the complex are the **exedra** (curved break in a row of columns) and **porticus** (covered walkway) of Trajan's Forum, separated by a **tufa** (porous limestone) wall and accessible through a grandiose central gateway.

The upper-level street, Via Biberatica, likely derived its name from the Latin word **biber** (to drink), hinting at the many alcohol-serving establishments catering to shoppers. The market offered diverse products from all over the empire: fruit, vegetables, fish, wine, oil and spices like pepper.

PLANNING FOR WAR AND PEACE

Many Roman developments in planning, building and administration kept order at home while helping to extend the empire abroad. At its height, the empire boasted a quarter of a million miles of roads that were essential to trade, transport and military conquest. These Roman roads were the outcome of a scientific approach to urban planning and zoning, and they were constructed from durable materials with drainage capacity. The **Via Appia** was a significant highway that linked Rome to outlying towns and cities such as **Capua**, **Brundisium** and **Taranto**.

Aqueducts were invented to solve the problem of transporting clean water into settlements for drinking, cooking, bathing and agriculture. Aqueducts showcased Roman breakthroughs in the discipline of hydraulics, manipulating gravity and the flow of liquid to great success. The first Roman aqueduct, **Aqua Appia**, was completed in 312 BCE, followed by others such as the **Aqua Marcia** and **Aqua Claudia**.

Similarly precise thought went into the design of **castrum** (military legionary encampments), which, like cities, had walls, gates, streets and accommodation areas.

REPUBLIC OF LETTERS

Greece was the defining influence on Roman literature, but over the centuries the Romans developed their own forms and genres. **Poetry** was a type of popular entertainment, with poets like **Virgil**, **Horace** and **Ovid** (pages 30–31) hugely respected.

Historical writing was also popular, although its reliability was often hampered by personal bias and the construction of a gripping narrative over fidelity to the facts. Even so, these accounts provide valuable insights. **Livy** (page 81) recounted Rome's history from its founding, and **Tacitus** (*c.*56–120 CE) was lauded for his critiques of certain emperors' excesses.

Epitomized by intellectuals like Cicero (page 51), **rhetoric** was another key literary genre and reflected the power of speeches to sway the public mind.

Cited as an influence by Shakespeare and Joyce, **Petronius** (27–66 CE) was an experimental writer before his time, depicting crazed, hedonistic characters and mashing up drama, prose and poetry in his ***Satyricon***. Some critics regard this as the first-ever novel.

THE HUMBLE WAY TO THE TOP

Seneca the Younger (*c.*4 BCE–65 CE) was a famed Roman politician, playwright and philosopher associated with the **Stoic** movement. Born in what is now Córdoba, Spain, he relocated to Rome when young, where he was instructed in rhetoric and philosophy. He saw nothing but continuity between public life and the life of the mind, and he rose to the office of close advisor to the emperor Nero.

His philosophical ruminations were contained in *Letters to Lucilius* and *On the Shortness of Life*, and they were concerned with what makes for a good life ethically and morally. Seneca's dramatic output is credited with progressing **Roman tragedy**. Works like *Phaedra*, *Thyestes* and *Medea* are praised for their nuanced insights into the human experience, grappling with the major themes of love, identity, power and vengeance.

He acquired significant wealth and power, prompting some to criticize him for hypocrisy, given his belief in simplicity and humility. He committed suicide after displeasing Nero and falling out of favour with the unstable emperor.

THE DETACHED HISTORIAN

Livy (59 BCE–17 CE) was an important Roman historian whose crowning achievement was the 142-volume ***Ab Urbe Condita*** (*From the Founding of the City*), which relates the history of Rome up to that time. From the 35 books that have survived, we can glean a good deal about Roman mores, politics and society.

Though a lot of his sources were secondary and oral, and could have been mythological, Livy's work combined detailed descriptions of the past – especially of events like the Punic Wars and figures such as Scipio Africanus – with moral and political analysis. He was especially concerned about what could be learned from Rome's past in order to deliver a better future for the civilization. Romans could only evolve, he argued, if they understood the virtues of their forefathers.

Unlike Seneca the Younger and others, Livy was not interested in participating in politics. He may have believed that his writings on history would retain a measure of impartiality for that reason.

PRACTICAL THINKING – MOSTLY

While Roman philosophy was indebted to Greek thought, it was very much adapted to suit the needs of Roman life and experience. It flourished during a time of crisis, between the crumbling of the Republic and the establishment of the Empire, when Romans needed new ideas to make sense of their turbulent lives.

In contrast to the supernatural preoccupations of other civilizations at the time, Roman philosophy was concerned with the practical and everyday, offering solutions to problems of a personal, social, political, scientific and economic nature. Many philosophers were also what we would today call physicists, biologists, anthropologists and social scientists. Hard-nosed **Stoicism** (page 85) is perhaps Rome's best-known philosophical school, with **Scepticism** (page 84) and the Greek-derived **Epicureanism** (page 83) also popular.

Romans imported **Pythagoreanism** from Greece, stripped some of its mystical elements away and made it into a creed focusing on mathematics, natural harmony and vegetarianism. More obscure philosophical sects included **Eleusians**, who believed in imbibing hallucinogenic substances at arcane rituals.

SIMPLE PLEASURES

Influential on the values and attitudes of especially upper-class Romans, **Epicurus** (341–270 BCE) was an ancient Greek intellectual for whom pleasure was the meaning of life, though not necessarily in the sense we would understand it today. For him, friendship, kindness and knowledge were all routes to pleasure and the good life. His motto "live unnoticed" advises us to seek happiness through balance and humility.

Epicurus was also ahead of his time as a **natural philosopher**, theorizing that the universe is composed of atoms shifting in a void, and rejecting religion and superstition in favour of a rational and scientific model of the world.

The Roman writers **Lucretius**, Horace and Cicero were all inspired by Epicureanism.

In decadent late Rome, Epicurus' ideas were grossly misinterpreted by some elite Romans, who used them as an excuse to overindulge in food, wine and sensual pleasures. Epicurus, who advocated a simple life of pleasure, would not have appreciated this.

THE DOUBTERS

A product of the intense intellectual culture of the **Hellenistic** period and the early Empire, Scepticism radically questioned certainty and the nature of knowledge. As Greek philosophers such as Pyrrho had before them, Roman Sceptics doubted whether we could trust what our senses tell us about the world, and therefore, we should not arrive at any concrete statements about it. **Sextus Empiricus** (late second–early third century CE) asserted that "The man who has doubts is the wisest."

Scepticism's methodology of constant doubt and debate helped the evolution of Roman knowledge in all areas, as reason and analysis took precedence over personal prejudice and superstition. Scepticism's emphasis on grey areas over black-and-white solutions and probability over certainty made it a useful guide to decision-making in tricky, contradictory political and military situations, as Cicero acknowledged.

However, in any creed there are always extremists and some Sceptics became paralyzed with indecision and paranoia because they had convinced themselves that the world did not exist and that no meaningful knowledge about it was available.

BE STRICT WITH YOURSELF

Emerging a little later than Scepticism, Roman Stoicism was preoccupied with the path to integrity, which involved bravery, prudence, wisdom and self-discipline. Not unlike the philosophies mentioned earlier, Stoicism favoured reason, science and interacting sensitively with nature.

Stoicism appealed up and down the social ladder. **Epictetus** (55–135 CE) made an unusual journey from slave to respected teacher and developed his own sub-branch of Stoicism that emphasized ethics, resilience and personal conduct. One of his students recorded his lectures in the books *Discourses* and the *Enchiridion* (*Manual*) before Epictetus was banished from Rome by the emperor **Domitian**, who was intolerant of intellectual dissent.

His ideas partly crossed over with those of the "philosopher-emperor" Marcus Aurelius, which were published in his *Meditations* (161–180 CE) and expounded on attitudes to death, human decency and virtue. Marcus Aurelius was pragmatic about the transience of existence and the connections between all human beings.

PUZZLINGLY PRAGMATIC

Lucretius (99–55 BCE) was a renowned Epicurean, and his most famous work, **De Rerum Natura** (*On the Nature of Things*), extolled the main points of the creed and mixed verse, science and philosophy. The book posits that **fortuna** (chance) makes the world work as it does rather than the actions of gods and that many of humanity's greatest discoveries were accidental, including the smelting of metal. Lucretius had a pragmatic attitude to death, claiming that it was just a natural part of the life cycle and should not scare us.

Almost nothing is known about Lucretius' life, making him a mysterious figure. The references to aristocratic ways and natural landscapes present in many of his works suggest that he was high-born and would have spent time on country estates.

One of his stranger theories is that of the **clinamen** (swerve) of atoms that ordinarily move in straight lines. This, for him, was evidence of free will in nature, which went against the Roman religious conceptions of fate and determinism.

LETHAL ENTERTAINMENT

The Roman fondness for power, one-upmanship and public achievement was manifested in spectator sport. Gladiatorial games were held in immense amphitheatres like the Colosseum, in which slaves and prisoners fought each other or against lions, tigers, bears, elephants, snakes and rhinoceroses.

The public placed bets on gladiatorial contests, and particularly riveting contests would enhance the prestige of the emperor who organized them. Winning gladiators would receive money, trophies and, if their career were successful overall, the **rudus** (wooden sword), which symbolized their liberty after a life of servitude. This way, gladiators could become free citizens.

Though most gladiators were effectively slaves, **Commodus** (161–192 CE) was an emperor who took part in gladiatorial combat. However, the fights were often rigged in his favour. Held mostly in the Circus Maximus, chariot races could be fatal, with drivers crashing to their deaths or being cut to pieces by **spinae** (spikes attached to wheels).

Less dangerous sports included athletics (including running races), boxing and wrestling, and took place during public festivals.

NOT EVERYONE WAS A FAN

The Roman writer Juvenal strongly disliked gladiatorial entertainment, writing, "The crowd is wild, the fighters sweat and bleed, and the spectators are mad for blood." He believed it brought out the worst in the Roman psyche, provoking people into bloodlust rather than appealing to their decency and humanity.

He warned that these spectacles distracted the masses from the important social and political problems affecting them and made them more likely to acquiesce to corrupt and incompetent leaders. More remarkably, for Romans of his time and status, he felt sorry for the gladiators and how poorly they were treated. As human beings, he argued, their lives should not be expendable for the entertainment of the better-off.

Exiled twice in his life – the first time for allegedly insulting a renowned actor – Juvenal was a satirist in a quite different sense to what we understand the word to mean today. He was not a comedian, as such, but rather an eloquent and trenchant critic of social norms that he deemed immoral or unreasonable.

SPORT, EXERCISE AND DISCIPLINE

Non-fatal Roman sport drew heavily on Greek disciplines that had been showcased by large events such as the **Ancient Olympic Games**. Roman running competitions fell into two categories that will be familiar to modern athletics enthusiasts: the **stadion** (a sprint) and the **diaulos** (a longer race over about 400 metres).

These contests took place in, among other venues, the **Campus Martius**, an army encampment in northwestern Rome whose facilities were also for civilian use. The Campus Martius evolved over several centuries but had its origins in the late Kingdom era. Roman military training included games and sports instruction, as being able to run, jump, throw, wrestle and box made for a useful skill set on battlefields, whatever the enemy, whatever the terrain.

Competition winners were given laurel crowns, and a successful athletics career could attract fame and fortune. While professional sport was only typically open to the better-off, a much wider sector of Roman society, including slaves and formerly enslaved people, participated in athletic training and entered amateur competitions.

HOME ENTERTAINMENT

For the less energetic there were parlour games, often played during private parties that also involved eating, drinking and socializing. A much-loved board game was **tabula**, in which players competed to be the first to move all their pieces around the board. Another was **ludus duodecim scriptorum**, the precursor to modern backgammon, played with dice (usually made from sheep and donkey bones), some counters and on a board with 12 spaces.

The most popular home gambling game was dice, and the highest roll, known as a **venus**, tended to win matches while losing rolls were referred to as **dog throws**. **Capita aut navia**, the forerunner of our "heads or tails", involved money wagered on whether a flipped Roman coin would land showing the **capita** (the head of a deity) or the **navia** (bow of a ship). Fortunes could be made or lost in a single evening.

Roman soldiers enjoyed **latrunculi**, also known as the **robbery game**. While we can't be sure of the rules, we know that each player had 12 pebbles and that the game may have been similar to modern checkers or chess.

WHAT A PERFORMANCE

Although the Greeks are credited with pioneering theatrical comedy, tragedy and other genres, the Romans took the art form to larger audiences and made their own contributions to the canon of great dramatic writing and production.

Plautus (254–184 BCE) adapted and updated a number of Greek plays for Roman tastes, engaging with themes of love, betrayal and class in a boisterous fashion. More subtle than that, the comedies of **Terence** (195/185–159 BCE) were renowned for their linguistic eloquence, relatable characters and moral sensitivity.

It must have been an awesome experience to watch a Roman play in one of the great venues of the time, such as the **Theatre of Pompey**, built in 55 BCE. Unlike Greece's open-air amphitheatres, Roman theatres had semi-circular layouts and tiered seating, allowing for improved visibility and acoustics.

Theatrical productions were spectacles, blending music, dance and pantomime, with the actors wearing elaborate costumes. Acting was male-dominated, with even female roles played by men. **Roscius** (126–62 BCE) was Rome's most celebrated actor, widely respected for his powerful emotional performances.

WILD ENTERTAINMENT

Wealthy Romans loved to organize large-scale hunts of bears, wild boars and even elephants and crocodiles. Teams of slaves and trained hounds joined the patrician hunters to track down and kill these beasts.

While most of these hunting parties ventured out into the countryside, many were staged in artificial arenas, with spectators looking on as aristocrats in their fine clothes threw spears at their quarry. However, such events often did not go as planned, with animals fighting back and injuring or killing their human oppressors. The bloodthirsty Roman crowd would look forward to such levelling of the odds.

Well-heeled Romans liked to keep pets to symbolize their wealth and status and as souvenirs of their travels around the empire. Monkeys were popular as companions, while large snakes and exotic birds such as peacocks would be displayed during feasts as emblems of power and masculinity. At these same events pet lions and leopards could be seen preening themselves or stalking about the place.

SYNCRETISM

Roman syncretism saw the merging of often disparate ideas, customs and conventions from the varied peoples within the empire. Artists and architects incorporated Greek columns and motifs, the **Pantheon** (erected around 27 BCE) epitomizing this. From the **Etruscans** (once based in what is now Tuscany), the Romans learned about vaults, arches, sewerage and drainage.

The great intellectuals of Rome were also influenced by Greece, imbibing and developing philosophies from **Stoicism** to **Epicureanism** for Roman purposes. Roman life was also shaped by **Carthaginian pragmatism**, a no-nonsense worldview devoted to business and practicality, and Celtic attitudes to nature.

Roman festivals, celebrations and holidays often borrowed agricultural and fertility rites from cultures that either predated Rome, like the Italian peninsula tribes, or that had been conquered by Rome.

The spread of Latin as the common language of the empire was seminal in the development of local tongues, yet also acted as a sponge for new words and phrases. In Rome's infancy, Latin absorbed elements of Etruscan, **Oscan** and **Umbrian** (from Italy), Celtic, **Phoenician** (in modern-day Lebanon) and **Punic** (Tunisia).

It was in religion that Roman syncretism was most apparent. As we have seen, the key Roman deities were strongly informed by Greek gods and goddesses. Moreover, **Isis** (goddess of magic, fertility, healing and maternity), **Serapis** (an Egyptian deity linked to the afterlife, among other things), **Baal** (a **Canaanite** storm god) and **Cybele** (a **Phrygian** maternal goddess) became incorporated into Roman traditions.

Roman soldiers were attracted to **Mithraism** for its emphasis on fraternity, loyalty and the struggle of good against evil. This strange sect was compatible with Roman beliefs and therefore tolerated, but it came originally from **Persian** legends, in which **Mithras** was a spirit of light and truth. Romans, however, saw his likeness in their deity **Sol Invictus**, who was responsible for the power of the sun. Mithraists performed arcane rituals, including the symbolic killing of a bull by Mithras (the **Tauroctony**), which represented life, death and rebirth. Mithraism faded as Christianity, itself an imported belief system, rose in the fourth century CE.

PARTY TIME!

If you were to be transported back through time to a Roman festival, you'd likely be wowed by its extraordinary colour, noise and vibrancy. Related closely to civic, agricultural and religious life, festivals existed to honour the gods, commemorate historical events and unite communities. **Animal sacrifices** were an essential part of any festival.

Saturnalia, held in December, was in tribute to Saturn, the god of agriculture. Attendees gave each other gifts, feasted on good food and temporarily reversed social roles, where slaves were treated as equals. Bulls would be slain during Saturnalia. The Jupiter-focused **Ludi Romani**, held in September, involved games and performances. Chariots raced, gladiators fought to the death, and vast crowds watched poetry recitals and theatrical performances. Pigs were ritually killed.

The Roman obsession with wine was marked by **Vinalia**, celebrated in April when the grape harvest came in. In the same month was **Parilia**, devoted to the pastoral goddess **Pales**. Both festivals featured rites to ensure a good crop.

CHAOTIC LOVE

One of the most flamboyant – and weirdest from our modern standpoint – festivals was the **Lupercalia**, celebrated each year on 15 February in honour of Lupercus, the god of fertility and shepherds. We know the following from accounts by Ovid and **Plutarch** (*c.*46– *c.*119 CE), the Greek philosopher who became a Roman citizen.

Specialist priests known as the **Luperci** congregated at the cave of Lupercal, where Romulus and Remus were purportedly nursed by a she-wolf. The Luperci then sacrificed goats and a dog, and they turned the skin of these beasts into strips called **februa**. Festival-goers would use these strips to gently strike women in the streets, as they assumed this boosted their fertility.

Lupercalia involved a lottery which would pair young men with young women for the duration of the festival. These brief unions often led to longer relationships and even marriage, in an act that went against Rome's usual conservatism about such matters.

Historians speculate that Lupercalia was the progenitor of our Valentine's Day but was much more disordered and less romantic.

INTEGRATION AND OPPRESSION

The Romans used various strategies to colonize different peoples. While occupying Athens in the 130s CE, Hadrian, a Graecophile, built a grand library to store Greek knowledge and completed the **Olympieion**, a plush shrine to Zeus. These edifices were a respectful testament to the cultural debt Rome owed Greece.

Hadrian established the **Panhellenion** (meaning "all-Greek"), a federation of Greek cities located in five Roman provinces, ruled over by an **archon** (senior official) and a council of delegates representing the member cities. He was also the first emperor to travel around the further-flung provinces of the empire out of intellectual curiosity.

The story is told of the Roman colonial regime in Gaul that decided to allow the locals to worship their deity **Lugus** since he seemed similar to Mercury; both were associated with trade and craftsmanship. But the Romans were mortified when they saw the Gauls painting and sculpting a bearded, well-built warrior – whereas Mercury was trim, peaceful and wore winged sandals.

Not all Roman attempts to absorb foreign cultures were as benign. In the first century CE, the Roman authorities banned the druidic practices of the Britons, regarding them as savage and pagan, and demolished groves on **Mona** (now the island of Anglesey) that were sacred to the Celtic populace. Roman armies also demolished significant temples in **Palmyra** (in the eastern Levant), Egypt and Anatolia.

Romans also tended to stereotype the communities they dominated. They mocked people from the Germanic region as slow-witted, **Iberians** for depending on donkeys for travel and trade, Gauls for drinking their wine undiluted and the Britons for wearing too few clothes for their cold climate and painting their skin blue with **woad** (a plant-based dye). "The Britons think themselves invisible when they're just blue!" was a gag from the time.

These subjugated peoples had their own views on the Romans, their insults and jokes often focusing on Rome's corruption, arrogance, excess, hypocrisy and bureaucracy. The Germanic tribes bemoaned their decadence and effeminacy, while the British chieftain Calgacius complained about Roman brutality: "They make a desert and call it peace."

THE WARRIOR QUEEN

One extraordinary woman who loathed Roman culture and values was **Boudicca** (30–61 CE) (Rome gave her the Latin name **Boadicea**). Queen of the Iceni tribe in what is now Norfolk, England, she fostered a grudge against the Romans after they annexed her husband **Prasutagus'** kingdom against his dying wishes. Boudicca's protests led to her public flogging and the rape of her daughters by Roman officers.

Her rebellion was personal and political, for many Celts were enraged about Rome's high taxes, their theft of local resources and their imposition of their religion and values on conquered tribes. In 60 or 61 CE, Boudicca allied with other disgruntled tribes and razed several major Roman towns, including **Londinium** (**London**) and **Verulamium** (**St Albans**), killing hundreds.

The defeats were hugely embarrassing to the Roman governor of Britannia, **Gaius Suetonius Paulinus**, who regrouped and finally routed Boudicca. She likely committed suicide before she could be captured. After death, Boudicca became an icon for Britannic cultural nationalism against the Roman Empire.

VIBIA THE BRAVE

Another strong woman – and a lesser-known yet key personality in Rome's difficult transition to Christian beliefs and culture – is **Vibia Perpetua** (182–203 CE). A Carthage-born aristocrat, Vibia had recently given birth to a child when she converted to Christianity. She and her associates came to be despised by the Roman authorities, Christianity at this time deemed subversive.

She and some fellow Christians, including her slave **Felicity**, were captured and ordered to renounce their faith on pain of death. Vibia refused, despite being tortured, and was pressured by her father to do as the Romans demanded. As recorded in her book ***The Passion of Perpetua and Felicity***, she had several visions which persuaded her to remain a steadfast Christian.

She was sent to a public arena to be killed by wild animals, as was the fate of so many Christians then. Somehow – miraculously, her followers might have thought – she survived being gored by a wild cow but was later executed by sword. Vibia is one of Christianity's early saints and **martyrs**, commemorated for sacrificing her life for her beliefs and for her unswerving bravery, fortitude and spiritual commitment.

LEAPS IN LANGUAGE

As Rome grew, so did Latin, its official language. Although its origins were obscure, spoken by relatively few tribespeople from the region of Latium in modern Italy, by the second century CE, there were 6–10 million Latin speakers across the Roman Empire.

Throughout its evolution, Latin absorbed influences from tongues spoken in adjacent territories, such as Greek and Etruscan, and many subjects of Rome's outer provinces were bilingual too.

The imperatives of government and officialdom led to the standardization of the **Latin alphabet** for legal and commercial documents, political proclamations, military communications and literary works. When the Western Roman Empire collapsed in the fifth century CE, Latin had become the formal language of Western civilization and intellectual inquiry.

A vital step forwards in the development of Latin was the introduction of the letter G by **Spurius Carvilius Ruga** around 230 BCE. This was an adaptation of the letter C to denote a new sound, which was crucial for accurately transcribing Latin words.

THE SOUNDS OF ROME

Music was a relatively inclusive aspect of Roman cultural life, as many singers and instrumentalists were current or former slaves. Their music could be heard in various settings: at theatrical productions, poetry recitals, religious ceremonies and festivals.

Choral singing as we know it today was likely invented in Rome, with groups of vocalists performing in honour of the gods and as part of religious rites. Solo singing was diverse enough to include bawdy ditties about everyday life and more refined lines of verse set to music.

Although dating back as far as 3000 BCE, the **lyre** was one of the primary string instruments of ancient Rome. U-shaped or triangular, the lyre often had five to ten strings and sounded soothing and majestic. The **tibia**, a reed pipe of varying lengths, could produce an alluring range of melodies. Military music, important to Roman morale, featured **cymbals** and **drums** played during parades and battles.

Sadly, not much written music from ancient Rome has survived. What we do know comes from the unearthed remnants of instruments and works of art depicting musicians in action.

BYZANTINE BRILLIANCE

After the culture of the Western Roman Empire fell into ruin (pages 136-7), the Byzantine Empire in many ways retained and built upon the achievements of its sister empire. The influence of Christianity is unmistakable in Byzantine mosaics, frescoes and buildings such as Hagia Sophia and the Church of the Holy Apostles (page 37), substituting images of Roman deities for Jesus, the **Virgin Mary** and the saints. Artistic realism was out of fashion, with imaginative depictions of divine light and heaven now the preference.

The Byzantines originated **iconography**, the creation of sacred images intended for Christian worship that supposedly brought one closer to God. The **Iconoclast Controversy** of the eighth and ninth centuries CE was a period of intense debate between artists and theologians about how most appropriately to create and venerate icons.

A new literary genre, **hagiography** (biography of a saint), emerged in the Byzantine era, epitomized by works such as **Athanasius' *Life of St Anthony***. Writers like **Theophanes the Confessor** produced exhaustive and eloquent histories of the Empire, its achievements and its conflicts.

A LASTING
LEGACY

It's time to revisit the question posed at the start of the book: "What have the Romans ever done for us?" From what you have read so far, Rome's significance to us today will be palpable from its advances in politics, law, engineering, language and much more. But how has Rome also inspired our ideas about everything from national identity to environmentalism, comedy to crop rotation? What are the most intriguing depictions of Rome in popular modern books, films and computer games? How historically accurate are they? And what have we learned from Rome *not* to do? Only one way to find out...

POLITICAL HERITAGE

Today, about 77 per cent of the world's countries are republics. Though the republic was a Greek invention, it was the Roman Republic that finessed the system's checks and balances, its separated and devolved powers, and its democratic accountability.

As a legislative assembly, the Roman Senate has influenced other such bodies across the world. The distinction we have today between executive, legislative and judicial power originated in the Roman Republic's sharing of authority between the Senate, lower-level politicians and popular assemblies.

Modern-day civic participation and political lobbying owe much to the Roman assemblies in which citizens and social and commercial alliances could express their opinions. Rome also casts a long shadow over the contemporary idea of the citizen as someone who educates themselves about the political issues affecting them and is thus able to make considered decisions in elections and referenda.

However, as we have seen, Rome was vulnerable to corruption and tyranny – just as our modern governments are, suggesting that democracy remains an unfinished project.

RIGHTS AND RESPONSIBILITIES

The twenty-first century's prioritizing of human and civil rights in frameworks such as the **Universal Declaration of Human Rights** is an outgrowth of **jus civile**, Rome's focus on citizens' rights. Rome's first effort at establishing a legal system was the Twelve Tables (450 BCE), which granted the right to a fair trial, the right of an individual to defend themselves at that trial and the right to own and inherit property.

Its other legal notions that will be familiar to us today include marriage rights, the right to appeal, regulation of debt and contractual agreements. Later in history, France was among several nations to enshrine such laws in its **Code Civil** (or Napoleonic Code).

Without Roman precedents, our property rights today would look very different. The Romans emphasized the importance of robust laws governing the ownership, protection and transfer of property for social order and prosperity.

Legal systems around the world extol the presumption of innocence until otherwise proved in criminal proceedings and permit defendants to be represented by an advocate. Originally, these were fundamental tenets of Roman law.

Not everything the Romans did regarding rights, crimes and punishments has endured – and that is not necessarily a bad thing. While many modern nations have abolished **retributive justice** through such punishments as the death penalty, many early Roman disputes were settled according to **lex talionis** (the law of exact retaliation), itself inspired by **Babylonian** legal measures. This vengeful approach to justice fell out of favour in later Rome, and financial penalties for civil offences were brought in, reflected in the compensation laws of our own time.

Livy recounts a tale – real, mythical or a mixture, we are not sure – that demonstrates how Roman thinking about lex talionis changed over time. The warrior **Horatius** returned home from fighting for Rome against Alba to find his sister grieving for one of the **Curiatii** brothers, his sworn enemies. He lost his temper and murdered her for treachery. Horatius was put on trial, with the punishment execution, but his father successfully argued for his pardon. In this instance, perhaps the offender got off too lightly.

LEGION LEGACIES

"For over a thousand years, Roman conquerors returning from the wars enjoyed the honour of triumph, a tumultuous parade... [But] a slave stood behind the conqueror holding a golden crown and whispering in his ear a warning: that all glory is fleeting." So said **George S. Patton**, iconic US general of the Second World War, of ancient Roman warfare. He was just one of many military minds shaped by the tactics, organization and discipline of Rome's armies.

Frederick the Great of Prussia's use of highly mobile units in the Silesian Wars (1740–63) was inspired by his studies of Roman battles, while **Napoleon Bonaparte**, who conquered large parts of Europe in the eighteenth and nineteenth centuries, developed **corps d'armée**, which were modelled on the self-sustaining and flexible Roman legions.

The engineering and design of siege weapons, forts and walls in later civilizations borrowed from Roman know-how, as do modern-day ballistics and mechanics. Our contemporary military hierarchies, training regimes, formations, supply lines and emphasis on teamwork have their roots in the highly professionalized armies and navies of the Roman Empire.

ENDURING EDIFICES

Had ancient Rome never existed, our towns, cities and buildings today would look very different. Concrete is ubiquitous in our built environment – and we have the Romans to thank for pioneering its use, even if our modern version is precast and reinforced in comparison. We also owe them the domes, vaults and arches of churches, museums and stately homes.

The Basilica of the Sacred Heart in Paris has a Christian Roman style to its semi-circular arches. **The Reichstag Building**, Berlin, had an **oculus** (an eye-like opening in wall or dome) added in the twentieth century, which owed much to that of the Pantheon.

Though themselves inspired by Greek expertise, Roman **Doric** and **Ionic** columns and pillars are typical of the neoclassical buildings we have today, including the **Lincoln Memorial** and the **US Supreme Court**.

Our roads are constructed using tunnels, levelling, land excavation and reclamation – but the Romans did all that first. Our plumbing and water management techniques evolved from Roman advances in hydraulics and aqueduct design.

KEEPING TIME

To resolve confusion caused by previous **lunar calendars**, Julius Caesar established the **Julian calendar** in 45 BCE. It introduced the **solar year** of 365 days that fell into 12 months, now familiar to us as our current **Gregorian calendar**. Before Caesar's reforms, there were only ten months in the year, but the great emperor added **January** and **February**.

Some of the names we still use for our months come from renowned Romans. **July** honours Caesar, while **August** does the same for the emperor Augustus. The Latin numbers from seven to ten inspired **September**, **October**, **November** and **December**.

The Julian calendar is also credited with creating the **leap year**, adding an additional day every four years to account for the 365.242 days it takes the Earth to orbit the sun.

Before Christ's time, there was a Roman festival of Sol Invictus on or around 25 December, and before our modern Mother's Day, the Romans paid tribute to motherhood at the **Hilaria** festival. Easter, Halloween and May Day may all have Roman origins too.

BUSINESS AS USUAL

It's not surprising that some aspects of Roman commerce and economics have survived. But did you know that our contemporary concepts relating to branding and advertising were forged in ancient Rome?

The quintessential Roman values of virtue, dignity, devotion, loyalty and self-control were represented in military and imperial insignia such as the eagle and the acronym **SPQR** (standing for **Senatus Popolusque Romanus**: the Senate and the People of Rome). Smaller organizations and businesses used branded posters, flyers and brochures in ways that would be familiar to a latter-day advertising executive. Merchants promoted their shops and market stalls with appealing slogans and eye-catching signs and paintings.

Trademarks and stamps, especially on Roman pottery, predated our own desire to know where goods come from, who made them and the level of their quality.

The webs of trade and industry that enable the production, exchange and distribution of goods across the world today have their origins in the Roman Empire's extensive road and sea networks, with the **Turkish** and **Hormuz Straits** today as important to commerce as they were 2,000 years ago.

If you think consumer culture began with **capitalism**, think again. Rome's spacious public markets offered buyers a dizzying array of goods from all over the world and, like modern malls, were places to socialize and look good in. Better-off citizens spent a lot of money on deluxe clothing, footwear and food as an expression of their social prominence and identity.

There are many similarities between the Roman **denarius** (silver coin) and the standardized currencies of the contemporary world, from the euro to the pound to the dollar. Trade across the empire flourished thanks to this uniform medium of exchange. The Roman Empire's mints were governed by the state, much like our central banking systems – both approaches have mitigated against fraud and counterfeiting.

From the days of the Republic, credit was a lucrative sector of the economy, with loans made to farmers and businesspeople on terms that are recognizable to our debt-dominated world today. While the earliest evidence of currency exchange has been found in Mesopotamian excavations, it was the Romans who first properly regulated such services.

WORKING THE LAND

Had we not learned some crucial lessons from the Romans about farming and agriculture, hunger and food shortages might be even bigger problems for us. "Food, feed and fallow" was the motto of Roman crop rotation, a trailblazing system of growing different crops at different times on a stretch of land to ensure fertility and reduce pests. Our farmers do the same today.

The Romans devised irrigation techniques such as canals, channels, tunnels and drainage systems in order to manage the water supply to their crops. Our contemporary drip and sprinkler systems, in which networks of tubes distribute water to the land, are indebted to these innovations.

Ancient Rome systematized the use of fertilizers commonplace in agriculture today. Despite the smell, animal manure was their most popular form, with composts of vegetables a close second. Our modern array of mineral fertilizers would have been highly familiar to a Roman farmer too.

Roman technological genius helped develop the equipment we use these days, such as the sickle for harvesting grains and the plough, which dredged up nutrient-rich soil and killed weeds.

ABIDING AESTHETICS

Our visual culture would be a good deal drabber without its Roman inheritance. The Renaissance's shift from depicting mystical experiences to a focus on the human form (as epitomized by the revolutionary works of **Michelangelo** and **Raphael**) had its origins in Roman realism and naturalism. We can, in turn, trace the same influence as far as twentieth- and twenty-first century CE artists such as **Lucian Freud** and **Kate Sierzputowski.**

The **baroque** period of portrait painting (seventeenth century CE) saw masterpieces by **Rembrandt** and **van Dyck** capture the power, status and indefatigability of their royal subjects – much like Roman pictures and busts of emperors, generals and statesmen had some 1,700 years earlier.

We may think of marble and bronze as the customary materials used in sculpture, but it was the Romans who refined this practice, along with elaborate methods such as **contrapposto**, where a kinetic mood is conjured by figures portrayed in a relaxed posture. Present-day sculptors, from **Antony Gormley** to **Richard Serra**, continue to explore such dynamics of space and form in their work.

AHEAD OF THE GAME

Roman sporting culture has had a significant impact on contemporary sports. Chariot races, often held in the Circus Maximus, were an early example of **team sport** and **fandom**. Like modern soccer, thousands of spectators would support different factions. Fans held similarly tribal attitudes to gladiatorial games and athletics events, whose league and tournament matchups inspired the organization of modern professional football (American or otherwise), rugby, basketball, tennis, athletics and the latter-day Olympic Games.

That the word gymnasium is derived from Latin offers a clue to what the Romans did for us in terms of sporting and fitness facilities. Contemporary gyms and aerobic, weight and cardiovascular training were begotten by ancient Rome's public spaces and stadia.

It is possible that modern football (whichever variety) and rugby evolved from the Roman game of **harpastum**, which was played with a leather ball and pitted two teams against each other. It could also get violent and cause injury.

MEDICAL HISTORIES

Roman doctors pioneered methods for treating wounds and fractures and were probably the first to use instruments such as the scalpels and forceps commonly employed in hospitals these days. The Romans knew about the pain-relieving effects of willow bark (the forerunner of the aspirin we have today) and the benefits of garlic for heart health.

Rome's sewage and public bath projects were rooted in an understanding that infectious disease was more likely to spread between unclean bodies and in unhygienic circumstances. These efforts inspired sanitation infrastructures built in the major industrial cities of the world.

Modern medical education can be traced to the practical training given to Roman doctors and nurses. Equally, our notions of medical ethics and law were shaped by the **Corpus Juris Civilis** (Body of Civil Law), compiled under the Byzantine emperor Justinian. This brought legal oversight to patient care and physicians' conduct and established informed consent for treatment.

Romans made great gains in medical observation and diagnosis, which is the basis of our contemporary **scientific method.**

LANGUAGE AND LONGEVITY

Few human languages can claim to have been so seminal as Latin. Its most obvious impact has been on the Romance languages, including French, Spanish, Italian and Romanian (which is the modern lingo that most closely resembles the Latin that Romans wrote and spoke). The grammatical structures (such as inflexion, in which the endings of words change to express different functions), phonetics and vocabularies of these languages are deeply indebted to that ancient tongue.

The international language today is English, which imbibed Latin words and phrases during the Roman occupation and, more indirectly, through the 1066 conquest by the French-speaking **Normans**. Sixty per cent of English words bear a close likeness to their Latin counterparts.

English scientific and legal terminology has borrowed directly from Latin, too, as phrases such as "Homo sapiens" and "habeas corpus" prove. Western biology and zoology progressed in the European **Enlightenment** thanks to the Swedish physician **Carl Linnaeus'** binomial naming system of plant and animal species. Thus, the common sunflower remains "**Helianthus annuus**" and the domestic cat "**Felis catus**".

PRESCIENT PENMANSHIP

Think of a great Western poet, novelist or dramatist, and they have likely been inspired by Roman letters. Indeed, our present-day **literary genres**, from tragedy to comedy to satire, were shaped by the achievements of Roman writers. Our whole definition of poetry – especially the epic kind – is the culmination of themes and devices pioneered by **The Golden Age** scribes (Horace, Virgil and Ovid) and augmented by later admirers from **Geoffrey Chaucer** to **Dante Alighieri**, **William Shakespeare** to **John Milton**.

The prose of today is equally beholden to Roman literature, with the scene setting, character development and thrilling narrative arcs of works such as Ovid's *Metamorphoses* evident in contemporary fiction.

The humanistic themes of literature – love, friendship, morality, loyalty, etc. – were hatched in ancient Rome. The attention to detail, chronological structures and persuasive registers of Roman rhetoric and history writing have strongly influenced more recent scholars, from **Edward Gibbon** to **Peter Brown**. And Roman poetic devices that remain popular include **chiasmus** (a reversal of the normal order of words for effect).

SHAKESPEARE AND ROME

Often regarded as the finest playwright since Roman times, William Shakespeare (1564–1616) was enthralled by that ancient society and was one of the first Western writers to fictionalize its most dramatic historical moments.

A meditation on violence and inhumanity, ***Titus Andronicus*** (1591) is about a vain and power-hungry Roman general who gets trapped in a brutal cycle of retribution. As the title suggests, ***Julius Caesar*** (1599) concerned the political conspiracy against the hubristic emperor, from its planning stages through to Caesar's murder and the power vacuum left by his demise. Its themes would have resonated with an Elizabethan audience quite used to intrigue, assassination and conflict in its own time.

In the classic "pride before a fall" narrative, ***Coriolanus***' (1605–6) eponymous hero becomes increasingly alienated from the Roman people and his own identity. Another tragedy, ***Antony and Cleopatra*** (1606–1607), stages the turbulent love affair between the Roman statesman and the Egyptian queen, exploring love, betrayal and the tensions between private desire and public ambition.

ROME BETWEEN THE PAGES

Ancient Rome's conflicts, tragedies, quirks and power struggles have long captured the imaginations of novelists. Here are some of the best fictional representations of Rome the Great.

- *The Last Days of Pompeii* (1834) **by Edward Bulwer-Lytton** – Remembered for his 30-odd novels and for coining the cliché, "It was a dark and stormy night", Bulwer-Lytton set this story in the horrific eruption of Vesuvius.
- *I, Claudius* (1934) **by Robert Graves** – Written from the perspective of Claudius and taking in events such as Caesar's assassination, *I, Claudius* set the benchmark for historical fiction.
- *The Eagle of the Ninth* (1954) **by Rosemary Sutcliff** – This thrilling novel for children focuses on the adventures of a young Roman soldier trying to find his father, who has disappeared in northern Britannia.
- *The Cicero Trilogy* (2021) **by Robert Harris** – An epic saga of the late Republic/early Empire period, its third book, *Dictator*, was hailed by the critic Stephanie Merritt as a "remarkable literary achievement".

SCREENING ROME

Rome's love of spectacle and aesthetics has translated very effectively to TV and cinema. Here are some recommendations.

- ◆ ***Ben-Hur: A Tale of the Christ*** **(1925) directed by Fred Niblo** – This groundbreaking silent movie's hero is Judah Ben-Hur, a Jewish aristocrat who encounters Jesus in his prime. Its breathtaking chariot race scenes influenced Hollywood for decades.
- ◆ ***Quo Vadis*** **(1951) directed by Mervyn LeRoy** – Set against the backdrop of the Roman conflict with the burgeoning Christian world, *Quo Vadis* is at its heart a love story between a Roman soldier and a Christian woman during the reign of Emperor Nero.
- ◆ ***Spartacus*** **(1960) directed by Stanley Kubrick** – Kirk Douglas' stirring performance as the rebel gladiator makes this a classic of the biblical epic genre.
- ◆ ***Gladiator*** **(2000) directed by Ridley Scott** - Combining gritty realism with blockbuster set pieces, this dramatic story of the avenging general Maximus helped refashion the Roman epic genre for the twenty-first century.

ROME ON THE SMALL SCREEN

Longer-form TV serials on Rome have had the time and space to address bigger themes and longer periods of history, and to dig deep into Roman psychology. Here's our pick.

- *I, Claudius* (1976) **directed by Herbert Wise** – This classy BBC miniseries is subtle and complex in its depiction of ambition and psychosis, with star turns from **Derek Jacobi, Sian Phillips** and **John Hurt.**
- *Rome* (2005–7) **created by John Milius** – This British-Italian co-production offers a kaleidoscopic vision of late republican/early imperial Rome, as experienced by two soldiers, Lucius Vorenus and Titus Pullo.
- *Britannia* (2018–21) **created by Jez Butterworth and others** – While it features a strong element of fantasy, *Britannia* offers some intriguing insights into life in Roman Britain and draws interesting parallels between belief, identity and nativism – then and now.

DIGITAL ROME

Given the importance of gaming to modern culture, it's no surprise that programmers have turned to ancient Rome for inspiration.

The widely acclaimed ***Rome: Total War*** series began in 2004 and has birthed numerous sequels. Players assume the duties of governors and generals, overseeing their towns and cities and sending their armies into real-time battles. The franchise owes much to the landmark ***Caesar III***'s (1998) emphasis on constructing buildings, allocating resources and protecting the citizenry.

The cinematically lush ***Gladiator: Sword of Vengeance*** (2003) belongs to the hack 'n' slash genre simulating gladiatorial combat, bearing some similarities with ***We Are Legion*** (2024) – an immersive RPG in which you play a Roman legionary on the front line.

A precursor to the state-of-the-art games above, ***Annals of Rome*** came out in 1986 and was lauded for its wargaming and political strategy elements. However, even by the primitive standards of the 80s, its simple graphics were slated by some critics.

SEEING IS BELIEVING?

For all the joy they have brought us, Rome-centred films are not always historically accurate. For example, it is unlikely that real gladiators and charioteers would have rippled with Russell Crowe-like muscles, given their basic diet of bread, veg and fruit. Nor would these men have worn elaborate armour, as you see in films like *Spartacus.*

Although Roman dress was relatively uniform, there were subtle distinctions between the clothes worn by rich and poor, a detail often overlooked in fictional representations.

Movies often make sloppy attempts to import Latin into their dialogue and scenery. In *Gladiator,* a sign on a building reads "LUDUS MAGNUS GLADIATORES", when it ought to say, "LUDUS MAGNUS GLADIATORUM".

In an early scene from the same film, a battle between Roman troops and Germanic tribes shows catapults and ballistae being deployed in a forest, but in reality, they were only used in sieges of towns and cities. And the naval skirmish in *Ben-Hur* is in many ways faithful to history, but it wrongly depicts the ships' oarsmen as slaves and incorrectly suggests that confinement to the ship's galley was a punishment of the time.

SICK OF MISREPRESENTATIONS

Some historical inaccuracies in fiction end up persuading people that they were in fact true. The Irish dramatist **George Bernard Shaw**'s (1856–1950) 1928 play ***The Apple Cart*** referenced a "**vomitorium**", a hole into which gluttonous ancient Romans would allegedly throw up food and wine – in order to make space in their bellies for yet more food and wine.

The problem is, there is no historical evidence for such an object. "Vomitorium" was in fact the term used to describe an underground passageway through which patrons would enter Roman amphitheatres. It was a very practical method of managing large, rowdy crowds and ensuring their safety as they moved around the busy venue – so quite a different thing to Shaw's conception.

Shaw was likely influenced by reading about the excessive consumption of certain emperors and aristocrats, who probably did vomit, given the amount of rich food and alcohol they devoured. But this didn't stop many people believing – and continuing to believe – that the vomitorium was where decadent Romans purged themselves.

ALWAYS LOOK ON THE BRIGHT SIDE OF LIFE

Our modern sitcoms often contain archetypal characters – the cynic, the buffoon, etc. – and these were commonplace in Roman theatrical plays and poems. The funny topical commentary our stand-up comics and television presenters offer would not be as eloquent and barbed without the influence of the Roman satirist Juvenal.

Our Roman forebears also liked puns. In Plautus' play **Amphitryon**, the god Mercury pretends to be a slave and plays with the Latin word "servo" ("to serve" or "I protect."). He says, "Ego servos servos servo." ("I, a slave, save the slaves.").

The Roman humorist **Macrobius**, who was alive around 400 CE, told the following joke: "Some provincial man has come to Rome, and walking on the streets was drawing everyone's attention, being a real double of the emperor Augustus. The emperor, having brought him to the palace, looks at him and then asks: Tell me, young man, did your mother come to Rome anytime? The reply was: She never did. But my father frequently was here."

FORWARD-LOOKING FOOD

We have learned from the Romans how to dry, salt and pickle meat, fish and vegetables for preservation purposes. Rome introduced an array of new cheeses to the empire, which look and taste like our contemporary Cheddar, Parmesan and Gouda. They also invented the technique of draining curds and putting them in moulds – an essential aspect of cheesemaking today.

Baking **sourdough** bread, adding yeast to a loaf and using beer to leaven your bread – these were favoured techniques of Roman bakers that have stayed with us. Our Worcestershire sauce is likely a descendant of **garum**, a fermented fish condiment. Mark McGowan, a culinary historian, argues that Romans' penchant for ingredients like garlic and olive oil laid the foundation for the latter-day **Mediterranean diet**.

At the height of Roman Britain, the occupiers had 10,000 men stationed across the country. A favourite food of theirs, quickly and easily cooked by local vendors, was **isicia omentata**, a minced beef or lamb patty served between two pieces of bread. Sound familiar?

SEXUAL IDENTITIES, PAST AND PRESENT

We may have put distance between our own societies and Rome's patriarchal structure, but Rome also serves as an important reminder that our acceptance of LGBTQ+ people is not new.

As we have seen, same-sex relationships were commonplace in Rome, though subject to class hierarchies.

Generally speaking, however, gay and lesbian Romans did not "come out" or openly identify with their sexualities in the way that is recognizable to us today. They kept their preferences and activities private, in keeping with the values of discretion and honour.

Only with the coming of Christianity in Rome was there a resurgence of intolerance towards LGBTQ+ people.

REINVENTING ROME

The contemporary historian **Christopher Kelly** has explored how, long after the fall of Rome, political and cultural leaders have tried to bask in the glory of that great civilization and use it to support their own aims.

In the late nineteenth and early twentieth centuries, UK academics regarded the story of Rome as instructive for running the British Empire. Boudicca was reclaimed as a British national heroine by **Thomas Thornycroft**'s iconic 1902 statue of her. But there were concerns that celebrating an anti-imperial rebel who dealt serious damage to the pre-eminent empire of her time might send out the wrong message to nationalist movements in Britain's own colonies.

Benito Mussolini asserted that his fascist dictatorship was the true heir to Roman power and glory, building the *Mostra Augustea della Romanità* (Augustan Exhibition of Romanness), which **Adolf Hitler** – who thought the Romans "breathtaking" – visited in 1938.

Kelly argues that post-war Hollywood injected American concerns into its "swords and sandals" epics by extolling the virtues of racial equality and having actors portray Nero as a Hitler- or **Stalin**-like figure.

EVERYBODY WANTS A PIECE OF ROME

Rightly or wrongly, more recent political leaders have referenced Rome's historical significance to justify their own ideas and policies. **Thomas Jefferson** (1743–1826), a Founding Father of the United States, frequently praised Roman governance, law and citizenship in his speeches and books. When waging the American Civil War, **Abraham Lincoln** (1809–65) invoked the Romans in support of retaining the Union of North and South. He called the US "a country whose great destiny might equal that of the great Roman Empire".

The Polish left-wing leader **Rosa Luxemburg** (1871–1919), who led an unsuccessful revolution in Germany in 1919, spoke of a choice between "ancient Rome, depopulation, desolation, degeneration, a vast cemetery; or, the victory of socialism".

When writing his famous "We Shall Fight Them on the Beaches" speech during **the Second World War**, British prime minister **Winston Churchill** (1874–1965) was thought to have been inspired by Roman bravery and patriotism. Former US First Lady and human rights campaigner **Eleanor Roosevelt** (1884–1962) warned that Americans, like Romans, could become "less willing to defend their freedoms".

The British politician **Enoch Powell** (1912–1998), a classics scholar, alluded to Virgil's *Aeneid* on the question of immigration: "Like the Roman, I seem to see the 'River Tiber foaming with much blood.'" Taking a different view, **Angela Merkel**, former Chancellor of Germany (1954–), has mentioned Rome in the context of contemporary refugee crises: "Since the Roman Empire... we know that splendid isolation does not help to protect borders."

Vladimir Putin (1952–) has referred to Moscow as "The Third Rome" in the belief that Russia is the last bastion of Christian civilization.

No stranger to controversy, in 2019, then-US president **Donald Trump** said in a press conference with his Italian counterpart **Sergio Mattarella**, "The United States and Italy are bound together by a shared cultural and political heritage dating back thousands of years to Ancient Rome." Critics pointed out that the US and Italy date back to 1776 and 1871 respectively, while ancient Rome ended in 476 CE.

LOOKING GOOD AFTER ALL THESE YEARS

While the way Romans dressed and made themselves attractive might strike us today as austere and simple, it has had subtle influences on our own fashion sense.

Contemporary ceremonial dress, like academic robes, has its roots in the elaborate togas worn by patricians, while garments such as the blouse and T-shirt came from the Roman tunic. Roman women moisturized their skin with creams, oils, honey and olive oil, and though we have abandoned the dangerous use of lead in make-up, rouge, eyeliner and lipstick remain popular. The Roman penchant for perfumes, including rose and lavender, has survived through to our current age.

Since the early twentieth century, American and Australian male students have held toga parties in which they wear the said garment while drinking heavily. After her husband Franklin was nicknamed "Caesar" by the press, Eleanor Roosevelt held a mocking toga party in 1934. The largest toga party on record took place in 2012 in Brisbane, Australia, attracting 3,700 revellers.

HOW NOT TO RULE

When it comes to judging who stands out today from Roman history as the most unhinged and unpleasant emperor of them all, the prize goes to **Elagabalus**, who reigned from 218–222 CE. Ascending to the throne when he was only 14, the Syrian-born Elagabalus is an object lesson in how not to rule a society.

He wasted a fortune on bizarre spectacles like uphill elephant-drawn chariot races and appointed incompetents to high office. Sex-obsessed, he was exploitative of men and women, giving official jobs to males based on the size of their penises before sleeping with them, and defiling a Vestal Virgin – normally a death penalty offence. He threw orgies in the Forum amid seas of rose petals.

Although there is less evidence for this claim, he personally tortured and disembowelled men in sacrifices. Cruelly, he chose victims whose parents were both still living to maximize their grief.

Unsurprisingly, Elagabalus alienated almost everyone. His own soldiers murdered him in his toilet, dragged his corpse through Rome and dumped it in the Tiber. "The life of Elagabalus, I should never have put into writing – hoping that nobody should know that he was emperor of Rome," wrote his biographer **Aelius Lampridius**.

INHERITING THE EARTH

Though ancient Romans were not facing the climate emergency we are today, they nonetheless protected the environment in multiple ways that will not seem outlandish to us now. Long before we started recycling metal and glass, the Romans were doing it, and a decision in around 120 BCE to reuse silver for coin minting helped to reduce lead pollution in the sea, which archaeologists have determined spread as far as Greenland.

Romans distinguished between different types of waste, and they disposed of the biodegradable kind in a **puticulum** (landfill). Inorganic refuse, such as pottery, was burned and applied in agriculture.

Roman public baths recycled water, a precious commodity at the time. In his 77–79 CE prophetic work ***Naturalis Historia*** (*Natural History*), Pliny the Elder posited a relationship between deforestation and flooding, and he warned about the ecological damage caused by extracting resources from the earth.

In an example of pioneering environmental legislation, Roman citizens could cut down no more than ten olive trees per year. Those who flouted this law could be fined heavily.

BACK AND FORTH

For all of Rome's achievements that are still with us, it's worth remembering that there was a long period of regression popularly called the **Dark Ages**, lasting from the fall of the Western Roman Empire in 476 CE until the tenth century. The American scientist **Carl Sagan** (1934–1996) described this miserable age as a "millennium gap... a poignant lost opportunity for the human species".

Political violence resulted from the break-up of the empire, with numerous power struggles between competing chieftains and warlords. Criminality thrived as law, order and a central political system all withered away. The crumbling of Roman commerce, banking and trade routes led to poverty and depopulation, and many societies in Europe reverted to subsistence farming.

The extraordinary cultural accomplishments that Rome had made were rolled back, with important books, works of art and feats of architecture lost or destroyed. Christian monasteries were the only communities that made an effort to preserve Roman ideas and values. Had they had more capacity, we might nowadays know much more about classical science, philosophy and literature.

Though originally a progressive force in Rome, the direction Christianity took during the Dark Ages suppressed moral freedom and intellectual inquiry. Relatively liberal attitudes to sexual relationships were phased out by an increasingly pious Christian Church.

The all-important Roman practices of plumbing and bathing went out of fashion in the Dark Ages, along with correct observations such as open pores on one's skin being healthy. For some odd reason, Dark Age people thought the pores should remain blocked lest fatal vapours attack the body. The consequences of less frequent bathing were disastrous, as disease spread and mortality increased. The only exception was monastic life, where devotion to God required purification with clean water.

There is by no means a consensus among historians about the Dark Ages. Some argue that the growing authority of the Christian Church provided checks and balances against monarchical rule and that, even if Europe was backward in those days, the Islamic world was rising thanks to new discoveries in mathematics, engineering and medicine.

CONCLUSION

The classical historian **Peter Burke** has said that we see history through the perspectives of those who "invent" it. It is true that, in the case of ancient Rome, it is often tricky to separate mythology from reality, metaphors from real events, and politically motivated slander from the truth about the reputations and behaviours of emperors, statesmen, generals, intellectuals, slaves, rebels and plebeians.

That said, historians and archaeologists have done a lot of important work to establish what is most likely to have been true about that time. Their accomplishments have allowed us to get a good measure of what it was like to live in Rome, how the civilization operated and expanded, and what it means to us today culturally, socially and politically. We see in it remarkable similarities and continuities with our own societies, but we have also learned lessons about mistakes that should not be repeated and prejudices best left in the dustbin of history.

How will Rome continue to inspire, influence, repel or puzzle us? What will it teach future generations who will occupy a world so radically different yet indebted to that civilization? As time passes, the thrill will be in the finding out.

FURTHER READING

TEXTS OF THE TIME

Selected Works by Cicero, translated by Michael Grant

The Complete Odes and Epodes by Horace, translated by David West

The Satires by Juvenal, translated by William Barr

The History of Rome by Livy, translated by Cyrus R. Edmonds

Metamorphoses by Ovid, translated by E. J. Kenney et al.

The Twelve Caesars by Suetonius, translated by James Rives

The Aeneid by Virgil, translated by David West et al.

MODERN TEXTS

Pompeii by Mary Beard

SPQR: A History of Ancient Rome by Mary Beard

Imperial Women of Rome: Power, Gender, Context by Mary T. Boatwright

Augustine of Hippo by Peter Brown

Rome: An Archaeological Guide by Amanda Claridge

The Atlas of the Roman World by Tim Cornell and John Matthews

Roman Women by Eve D'Ambra

Spectacle in the Roman World by Hazel Dodge

Cicero: The Life and Times of Rome's Greatest Politician by Anthony Everitt

The Rise of Rome: The Making of the World's Greatest Empire by Anthony Everitt

Pagans and Christians by Robin Lane Fox

The History of the Decline and Fall of the Roman Empire by Edward Gibbon

The Complete Roman Army by Adrian Goldsworthy

The Fate of Rome: Climate, Disease, and the End of an Empire by Kyle Harper

Rubicon: The Last Years of the Roman Republic (trilogy of works) by Tom Holland

Shopping in Ancient Rome: The Retail Trade in the Late Republic and the Principate by Claire Holleran

The Brothel of Pompeii: Sex, Class, and Gender at the Margins of Roman Society by Sarah Levin-Richardson

The Emperor in the Roman World by Fergus Millar

The Darkening Age: The Christian Destruction of the Classical World by Catherine Nixey

The Assassination of Julius Caesar by Michael Parenti

The Corrupting Sea by Peregrine Horden and Nicholas Purcell

Agrippina: The Most Extraordinary Woman of the Roman World by Emma Southon

The Spartacus War by Barry Strauss

Latium: Prelude to the Roman Kingdom by Peter Tattersall

Class Struggle in the Roman Republic by Alan Woods

Twelve Voices from Greece and Rome: Ancient Ideas for Modern Times by Christopher Pelling and Maria Wyke

WEBSITES AND PODCASTS

www.ancientromelive.org

www.english-heritage.org.uk/learn/story-of-england/romans

www.romeactually.com

The History of Rome Podcast with Mike Duncan

The Partial Historians with Fiona Radford and Peta Greenfield

The Ancients – History Hit

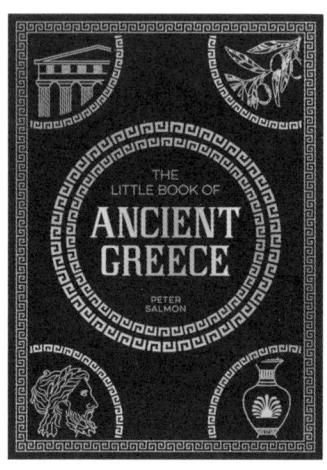

THE LITTLE BOOK OF ANCIENT GREECE
Peter Salmon

Paperback • 978-1-83799-535-6

If you've ever been curious about the rich culture and vibrant history of Ancient Greece, dive into this small but mighty tour of the highlights of this epic civilization. From warfare and politics, to art, culture and everyday life, uncover the key events, people and trivia you need to know to understand this remarkable period of history.

THE LITTLE BOOK OF WORLD MYTHOLOGY
Hannah Bowstead

Paperback • 978-1-80007-176-6

Step into a world of gods, heroes and monsters. This handy guide offers readers an accessible introduction to the major world mythologies, their origins, foundational stories and key mythological figures. If you're looking to enrich and expand on your understanding of world history, religion and culture, then this book is an ideal starting point to fill your mind with stories of wisdom and wonder.

Have you enjoyed this book?
If so, find us on Facebook at
Summersdale Publishers,
on Twitter/X at **@Summersdale**
and on Instagram and TikTok at
@summersdalebooks and get in touch.
We'd love to hear from you!

WWW.SUMMERSDALE.COM

Image Credits